To Ed,

With
Love

The Journey of a Priest to find himself, his God and his own wisdom

• •

by Bill Whittier

The title of the cover photo is "The Journey". It was taken by Margaret Van Kempen, OSB: St. Benedict's Monastery; St. Joseph, MN 56374.

This photo is appropriate because of the events that occurred in ancient geologic time to the present. Fr. Bill's journey has been formed, changed and renewed, as the eroded rocks and mountains have been formed, changed and renewed. Today the St. Louis River flows through Jay Cooke Park and into Lake Superior in Duluth. The modern day bridge crosses the river in the distance and trees are growing out of the rocks. In Fr. Bill's life journey the bridge is the bridge of love crossing over the troubled waters of our lives and our world.

The Journey of a Priest to find himself, his God and his own wisdom

by Bill Whittier

Caritas
Communications

ACKNOWLEDGMENTS

I want to thank Hal and Sidra Stone and all my many mentors for their inspiration and guidance on my Life Journey.

Thanks to Leigh Caplette from Menno Travel Service of Minnesota. Without Leigh's travel wisdom, expertise and generosity Fr. Gulliver's ship probably would never have left dry dock in the USA. Thanks to him all travel arrangements were well planned and executed. Fr. Gulliver never got stranded and always arrived safely home.

Thanks to Ken LaBore my webmaster and computer teacher for his expertise and generous service. Lots of computer learning was needed to complete this autobiography And much patience was needed by Ken.

Thanks to Rick O'Connell, the computer whiz behind the scenes always ready to help both Ken and I.

For Leigh, Ken and Rick I became "the Priest pest" but they did not mind and were always there for me when I needed them.

Thanks to my childhood friend Cletus Rotty and his generosity and expertise being my personal photographer.

Thanks to Vicki Mc Nally and her daughter Bridget for their creative promotion and distribution of my autobiography.

Thanks to Kelli Stohlmeyer for finalizing our cover design.

Thanks to David A. Gawlik and Caritas Communications for guiding this autobiography into its published form.

ENDORSEMENTS

"The autobiography of Bill will show the reader how closely Bill's path and the Path of Kripa soaked in and blended together the presence of Mother Teresa. We are deeply grateful to God for sending Bill like an Albert Schweitzer to the afflicted of Addiction in India. May God bless him with a long life and well being."

Fr. Joe Pereira, Managing Trustee, Kripa Foundation, India

"I feel very honored to be asked to endorse your book. From our friendship I see you as a person open to self exploration, honesty, respect and tolerance for people of different temperaments and cultures."

Rani Raote, Psychotherapist practicing in Mumbai India.

"We cannot know how long we will have in this world. But we do know we are on a journey. Life is constantly changing and moving on. I have been a fellow priest and friend with Bill Whittier for over 30 years. I know Bill understands and writes about Journey. In this book he shares the story of his life journey and he offers many good hints for anyone else who is serious about their life journey be they priest, layperson, young or old. In this time and place I commend this book as a companion on your life journey."

Father Roger Pierre

"For us therefore who are on this life journey, I would recommend my friend and mentor's book—Fr Bill's Life Journey. He shares with us the story of his life journey. In doing so he offers many useful hints for anyone else who is serious about life journey. Those who might find the book helpful are Christian Pastors and Laypersons, Doctors, Teachers, Therapists, persons interested in holistic health and healing, young or old members of all different world Religions, those in recovery or in need of recovery or any PERSON young or old serious about their life journey and their spiritual growth. I have been richly blessed not just going through the book but being closely associated with the author in different facets of life."

Dr. Christian Ogoegbunem Isichei BM, BCH, MSc, FMCPath

Caritas Communications
Thiensville, Wisconsin 53092
dgawlik@wi.rr.com
414.531.0503

Printed in the United States of America.

Cover by Kelli Stohlmeyer, kelli@kel-i-design.com

Whittier, Bill

The Journey of a Priest

ISBN 0966822846 / 978-0-9668228-4-7

DEDICATION

I dedicate this book to my Whittier-Molitor family of origin and to my family of choice who all share life with me on our living space ship planet earth.

I also include those who hold a special place in my heart–namely those in recovery or searching for recovery and those helping others find and remain faithful to recovery.

I also include with special thanks all my friends and enemies who have been my life teachers on my journey of love. Thanks for Your patience when I was many times a slow learner.

CONTENTS

PREFACE

As I wrote and reflected on my *Journey of Love* I asked the question, who might want to read this autobiography?

HERE IS MY ANSWER:

Those with mentors or searching for mentors like John Henry Cardinal Newman, Mother Teresa, Teihard de Chardin, Thich Nhat Hanh, Bede Griffiths, Ed Hays, Ghandi, Matthew Fox and many others exploring the mystery of the Risen Cosmic Christ in their lives and in the universe.

Those following or desiring to follow the teaching of Hal and Sidra Stone on the psychology of selves, voice dialogue and the aware ego.

Those following or desiring to follow the discipline of Christian meditation as taught by John Main and now by Laurence Freeman, OSB.

Those in recovery or seeking recovery from alcoholism and other addictions following the 12 steps of AA.

Those exploring a possible vocation to the Catholic priesthood.

Those exploring and questioning the direction of the Catholic Church in our modern day world.

FOREWORD

We have known Fr. Bill Whittier for 36 years. We met at the very beginning of the Center for the Healing Arts in Los Angeles, California, when he attended the summer conference on energy healing. At that time, it was an opening into a new world for Fr. Bill and he never stopped coming to these Center programs; he was always curious and always open to new ideas. He drank up the new knowledge and the new experiences in a most amazing way and—even as he did so—he remained true to his Catholic heritage and to his calling as a priest. This remarkable ability to hold potentially irreconcilable opposites is a quality that has marked Fr. Bill's journey at each stage of his life.

As time passed and he explored many new ways of working with people, Fr. Bill became involved in our work, Voice Dialogue, which was taught at the Center. He ultimately began to practice Voice Dialogue on his own, in his pastoral counseling, and many years later, was to bring it to many parts of the world and introduce it to many people who otherwise would never have had access either to our work or to the ideas behind it. We are extremely grateful to Fr. Bill for this opportunity to contribute to these far-flung communities.

During this time of exploration, Fr. Bill's ongoing interest in the field of addiction led him to Hazelden where he honed his skills as an expert in their approach to the treatment of addictions. He was able to combine these two areas of interest and expertise—again under the aegis of his calling as a priest—and to move forward in a most original and creative fashion at a time in life when many of his contemporaries might be settling down into a life of ease and retirement.

Mentors have abounded in Fr. Bill's life and, no matter how diverse their approaches to life, he has always found ways of combining their insights and teachings into something new. And each has contributed something special to the richness of Fr. Bill's own work.

All these explorations came together and his second career began after his 65th birthday. Fr. Bill began to travel around the world bringing consciousness work to a wide-ranging group of teachers, nuns, priests, counselors, and addicts. He became a kind of Pied Piper of consciousness, carrying his work to many different settings around the world—all of them in some way connected to the work of the Catholic Church.

This book is the story of Father Bill, The Traveling Priest. How did his changes come about? How did Bill maintain his deep connection to the church itself when he took on a second career of consciousness teacher in the midst of the wild days of the nineteen-seventies and eighties when so many wonderful young men were lost to the church during those years of powerful change in the world? This book gives a picture of one man's journey.

Father Bill is still very much a priest but his is really a different kind of priesthood than anything we have every seen. We asked him to write this book because it would have been sad to have his particular story lost. We each have our stories and it is these stories that are possibly the greatest gifts that we can pass on to others. They are the stuff of life and each is unique and irreplaceable.

Fr. Bill has been called a "soul shaker" and a "world changer"—he is someone who can bring to others a new way of looking at life without losing the priceless treasures of tradition. Instead of separating himself from his church and his calling, Bill simply learned to sing his own song within the context of the church and what a song it has been.

Fr. Bill has lived an inspiring life, and his life story is a gift! Enjoy!

Hal Stone, PhD and Sidra Stone, PhD,

Albion, California

http://www.voicedialogue.org

Hal and Sidra Stone my Teachers, Mentors and Friends who play a very important role in my Life Journey and have encouraged me to write this autobiography.

CHAPTER ONE
A Priest's Journey

"We shall not cease from exploration and the end of all our exploring will be to arrive where we started and know the place for the first time."

T.S. Eliot – "Little Gidding" in Four Quartets

L ife is a journey to find ourselves, to find our God and find our own Wisdom. This is the Journey of my life and I suggest everyone's life.

This is the journey of William Owen Whittier born on September 25, 1934 in the small town of Farmington, Minnesota, USA—ordained a Roman Catholic Priest for the Archdiocese of St. Paul and Minneapolis on February 19, 1961. At the age of 65 and even before rather than be considered "retired," I was "refired" by the Spirit of the Living God of this magnificent universe which is our gracious home. As Bill Whittier, a Catholic Priest, I am also a world teacher and counselor in the field of chemical dependency. Besides this I am a world psycho-spiritual teacher and counselor helping people grow psychologically and spiritually. As an *Aware Ego*, I keep the balance and hold the tension of the opposites of my many selves. The *Aware Ego* has been with me on my life journey even though at the beginning I was unaware of it.

The *Aware Ego* is a process of consciousness that stands between opposites and knows the opposites and experiences their unique energy. As we hold the tension of the opposites with the *Aware Ego* we are connected with the cave of our heart where we experience our vulnerability, our uniqueness as a person and our connection with the God of our understanding. Also by knowing both opposites we have choice and freedom between the opposites. Most of life at least on my journey is not black or white but gray. The *Aware Ego* helps us stand in that gray area and make life choices which come from our own vulnerability, spirituality and wisdom that do not polarize but calls for understanding and respect from both opposites.

When I travel around the world I introduce myself in this way. There are three Bill's from the USA –Bill Clinton our ex president; Bill Gates the Microsoft multimillionaire and me Bill Whittier. I am not as wealthy as the other two but I am "Whittier." A priest at the Archbishop's house in Imphal in N.E. India said," Hold on a minute you have forgotten another bill from USA, the dollar bill." But lest I forget there is a fifth Bill. This Bill is Bill W. who those of you in recovery would recognize as the founder along with Dr. Bob of Alcoholics Anonymous. I suggest persons living with alcoholism and other addictions need to be grateful to Bill W. Without his discovering and giving us the 12 Steps of A.A. for recovery most alcoholics and addicts would be today either in jail or dead. As I look around the USA and travel in Africa, Ireland, India and the Philippines I find this is so true. There are many jails and prisons full of alcoholics and addicts being punished rather than receiving healing. There is a basic education statement that needs to be proclaimed loud and clear all over our home planet earth. The statement is this: PERSONS LIVING WITH ALCOHOLISM AND ADDICTION TO DRUGS ARE NOT BAD PEOPLE WHO NEED PUNISHMENT BUT THEY ARE SICK PEOPLE WHO NEED HEALING.

Many of my friends have encouraged me to write this autobiography. They feel I have important hints of wisdom to offer others as they make their life journey. If you join me on my journey you may find some hints of wisdom for your unique life journey. Hal Stone and his wife Sidra who come from a Jewish background have always respected my priesthood. With patience, wisdom and generosity they have observed, nurtured and challenged my spiritual and psychological growth for thirty years. They have encouraged me to write this autobiography and have been my teachers, mentors and friends. They are the originators of the theory of the Psychology of the *Aware Ego* and the process of *Voice Dialogue*. You will meet them on our journey together. Hal offered a number of titles for this book: "*Adventures of a Wandering Priest*;" "*God Didn't Tell Me It Could Be So Much Fun*;" "*New Options in Becoming a Priest*" and others. Hal suggests, "It needs to be as personal as you can make it. Don't be form bound. Have a good time. Have fun." To be honest if it wasn't for Hal's encouragement I would not have taken on this challenge. Interesting enough before he challenged me to write I was encouraging him to write a much-needed book on his favorite subject of energy. I mentioned to his daughter Judith who is presently meeting a serious cancer challenge that maybe your father has me writing the book I wanted him to write. She commented that knowing her father this could be very true.

Ed Hays also a mentor and teacher of mine but not to the extent of Hal and Sidra was not too encouraging when I asked him about writing my autobiography. But then Ed went on to say, "Go with caution. Your life is the Whittier Gospel! The Good News according to William tells of the mysterious way the Divine Mercy has and is working in and through me, using my gifts and my stupidities, my achievements and mistakes to usher in the Kingdom of God's Love."

Along with these tidbits of advice and encouragement I need to admit I was not sure I had the patience to write and do all the hard work to get my autobiography edited and published. Nevertheless here I am writing and inviting you to join me on my life journey which essentially I feel is your life journey as well. So come join me as we begin my life journey back in the small town of Farmington, Minnesota, USA.

My family - Mother Jeanette - Father Leslie left to
right; me Bill, Charlotte, Larry, John behind Larry

CHAPTER TWO

Growing Up In Farmington
1934-1952

"Cor ad cor Loquitur"
(Heart speaks to heart)
"Lead kindly light."

John Henry Newman

5

These two quotations from my mentor John Henry Newman reflect the energy that I grew up with as a young boy. My mother was a faithful practicing Catholic and my father was a non–practicing Methodist. Religion was respected and encouraged. My father honored my mother's choice to raise their children in the Catholic Religion. Looking back now I would say the energy around our home reflected that religion was important; God was "kindly light." The sharing of the heart, honoring and listening to each other's heart was more significant than the head.

My father's Methodist side of the family was large. His mother and father lived in Farmington with most of his brothers and sisters and their children. These would be my uncles and aunts and cousins. My mother's Catholic side of the family was small. Her father and mother lived in Farmington along with my great uncles and aunts. My mother had one sister Charlotte who studied at the University of Minnesota. While working at Glacier National Park she met her future husband from Wyoming. She married him and since then they have lived in different parts of western USA and out of the country. She never came back to Farmington except to help my

Wedding picture of my Mother and Father - The beginning of their and my Journey of Love

grandmother and my mother take care of my grandfather Molitor who died of cancer in 1941 at the age of 63. Her son Bob was my age and came with her. He and I attended Second Grade together and developed a special bond of friendship still strong to this day, 67 years later. You can see my Catholic side of the family was rather small and my Methodist side was very large. Happily we all got along well together. I was blessed when growing up to have known all four of my grandparents. As I reflect back from my living in India I could see we were something like an "Indian Joint Family" we all lived in our separate homes but had many of the blessings of a joint family.

Father David Moran, our pastor in my early years of growing up was a retired army chaplain. He was friendly, gregarious and loved people. Father Moran lived and shared with the whole community this same energy that our common God was not a punishing God but was kindly and light. We connect with each other with the heart rather than theological discussions and arguments from the head which often separate rather than unite. This was the spirit of our parish church and expressed itself in many ways in the whole community of Farmington. Father Moran died at the age of 63 when I was ten years old. He has a large memorial marker at a central location in the Farmington Catholic Cemetery. I share the inscription, which gives a sense of who he was and how well he was respected. Father David Moran—1881–1944. Pastor/Humanitarian/ Legionnaire. Dedicated to His Memory by the Legionnaires of the State of Minnesota. In those days the Catholic and Protestant Cemeteries where next to each other but there was a fence between them. Now the fence is down and the openness reflects the ecumenical spirit of the different religions. There is one big Christian Cemetery and we are one big Christian Family.

Compared to now the public school and our parish church had a very ecumenical spirit of openness and sharing. Our parish church was just across the street from the public school. We had release time from the public school to attend religious education classes. If there were funerals in our church we could obtain permission to serve the funerals and be excused from classes. I enjoyed getting out of school to serve. This at times was to the envy of some of my Protestant friends. I was exposed at an early age to funerals and the death of many older members of my family. I learned at this time that death was not to be feared and to fear to die was to fear to live. This same ecumenical spirit was seen at Christmas. Christmas was celebrated in the public schools with a common spirit of love and light with the singing of Christmas carols, a Christmas Crib and other Christmas art.

When I was in my early grade school years young Benedictine Sisters came down from St. Joseph, Minnesota, their motherhouse, for summer religious instruction. They taught us the necessary Religious education we needed to prepare us for our First Communion and Confirmation. We were surrounded by these young sisters, full of fun, a love for life, and the energy of a loving God. I always remember and have a special place in my heart for Sister Mary Anthony Wagner who was young, tall and beautiful. She was later to become the head of the Theology Department at the College of St Benedict in St. Joseph, Minnesota. When the St. Paul Priory was established, the local Benedictine community separated from the Motherhouse in St. Joseph, Minnesota. The Saint Paul Priory then provided for our religious education needs with some equally loving, retired Benedictine Sisters from the Priory. These sisters were in charge of our religious education in our high school years. They lived in a small convent provided for them by our parish. Their door was always open to visitors and to us as children. We would, on occasion, go for breakfast after serving morning Mass. I always waited for the extra chocolate we got to top off our breakfast. To this day I like a little chocolate to top off my breakfast.

As teenagers we did not always treat the Sisters with the respect they deserved. We would talk and fool around in class and not always come on time. But in spite of our often-disrespectful behavior the energy they sent out to us was kindly and light, reflecting the God they loved and served. They taught us to love and serve this same God. As I look back now MOST of us have done well in life and are still active Catholics. Two of my favorite Sisters who I remember with affection to this day were Sister Ignatia Zervas and Sister Adelia Schmitt.

I was second oldest in a family of four children. John was the oldest. I was one year younger and my sister Charlotte one year younger than I. Our "baby" brother Larry was two years younger than Charlotte. Dr. Sanford our family doctor delivered babies at home. I still recall at age three standing outside my mother and father's bedroom waiting for the news of the birth of Larry.

Grandmother Molitor - left to right - Bill, Larry, John, Charlotte.

My two brothers and sister were much more athletic than I was. I did better scholastically in school than they did. I played weak side tackle on the football team but did not like the violence of the sport. However I enjoyed the mixture of guys on the team and a wonderful coach in Stan Nelson. Stan again reflected in his life and his leadership a God that was kindly and light always giving us positive encouragement to be the best player and team member possible. I remember one day I made a fantastic down field block, as the weak side tackle. As a result of this block Bob Kirchner our fullback and my classmate made the winning touchdown. After the play Coach Stan Nelson came over and patted me on the behind and said Bill you are my best weak side tackle. I did not think I was but I became so in my senior year.

The heart to heart with a love for life and fun was important for communication amongst the team and with Stan Nelson our coach. I was not the big football star but was elected in my senior year to be the home coming king. I feel my heart to heart openness, my friendly spirit and love for life and maybe the girls too got me elected as home coming king. I was not the typical big football hero. In "The Tiger of 1952," our yearbook published by the Senior Class next to my picture was written," Tall, dark and shy, with a gleam for the girls in his eye."

Rather than go out for many sports in high school I chose to work at the local National Tea Store, which sold much more than tea. It was the local food market in town. This seems again to me to reflect the importance for me of enjoying people, being with people and helping people. The job also provided me with the opportunity to earn some money for my personal needs such as clothes and to save some money to pay my own way for college. I was encouraged to go out for baseball. The coach at the time suggested I would make a good pitcher but my interest was not there. I did play "B Team" Basketball and backyard basketball but I was not good enough for the "A Team" as both my brothers John and Larry were. If girls had the opportunities for sports like they have today my sister would be right in there with the best of them. This choice of the job over sports was an example as I look back of my *Aware Ego* in action weighing both opposites and making the choice for work rather than sports. Many of my classmates chose the sports. I enjoyed the working in the Food Market and had many different jobs, which I found challenging and fun. I worked at the meat counter, the produce counter, stocked shelves and ran the cash registers which were not so computer friendly as they are today. They were more difficult to operate and you had to make sure you rang up items correctly. At the end of the day you had to make sure your cash register would balance out correctly or spend long hours after work finding the error. Unlike our large super markets today, we were expected to be available and provide personal service and advice when needed to the shoppers.

Even though at the time I did not even know who John Henry Newman was his two simple prayers reflected much of whom I was and the energy I carried in my life. I loved to dance and loved the girls. However I do not think this was part of Newman's interest. There were four or five of us guys and gals who loved to dance. We would go around to the local dance halls having wedding dances and sneak in. When we could we sometimes would make ourselves look old enough to have a beer. All of this reflected my love for life, for music and love for people. These personal qualities I feel prepared me in my heart for the priesthood and for my eventual love for counseling and helping people. Along with this I had a healthy image of God who was kindly and light. A friendly heart and smiling face was important in relating to people and to God and very important in working with people and serving people in the Food Market.

Our town of Farmington Minnesota was in the middle of a very fertile farming area with a population then of about 2000. We did not farm but our neighbors farmed. The town with all its mixture of people and religions and public school education reflected again that the God of our lives was kindly and light and inclusive. I would say the town was made up of about one fourth Catholics and three fourth Lutherans, Presbyterians, Methodists and some Episcopalians. There were no Jews in our community or black Americans at the time. About half of our senior class came from farms in the neighboring areas or smaller towns nearby who had no high school. Our senior class was made up of 48 students with about one fourth Catholics. There were 21 teachers for junior and senior high. With all of our differences we got along well with each other. Again the heart was important for living life, enjoying life and connecting with our God.

After Father Moran died some of the succeeding pastors were not so ecumenically inclined. Some were dealing with the disease of alcoholism, a disease I would meet later on as a priest and counselor. Another addiction disease seduced my father into being involved in gambling, which would be seen today as a disease and an addiction. The gambling took place in the back smoke filled room of our local pool hall. We as youth could play pool and hang out in the front area. The back room was off limits to us. I do remember many times I would go back in the smoke filled room to call my dad home for supper or some other family need. His losing money as most gamblers do in the end and staying up late at night cost my dad his good civil service job in the local post office. This put our family in debt and was an added burden on my mother. She already at the time was working to make financial ends meet in our family. The more detailed information about my father's loss of his job and what was involved was kept from us children. It was an embarrassment to my mother and to all of us. After this my dad needed a job so he came to work with me at the local National Tea Store. We worked well together but the heavy burden of stocking shelves, going up and down the basement stairs carrying heavy boxes, worrying about supporting his family plus being a pretty heavy smoker developed into a heart attack. This was another added burden on my mother and all of us to some degree. But it also drew us together by all of us pitching in to help the best we could.

Later on my father got a job as supervisor with the Herb–Shelly Company in Farmington where I also then worked. Gilmore T. Schjeldahl better known as Shelly invented in his basement a plastic bag making machine and the first of its kind. Shelly was a creative genius and a beautiful generous man. He moved from his basement into the factory, which was in Farmington from 1949 to 1955. My dad and I worked together well and I feel this brought us both into a deeper personal relationship. My father and I both were well loved there and did good work. Shelly was a wonderful boss and became a dear friend as well. I always remember to this day one of the women who worked there used to kid me about marriage. Her bit of wisdom was, "marry the first time for money and then the second time for love." At that time in my life as I write this I have married for neither.

As far as I remember my father left his gambling habits at this time. Only later understanding the disease concept of alcoholism and its genetic connection, I came to see how the alcoholism and other addictions like gambling ran though my father's side of the family. They are still surfacing in my cousins. My father's younger brother who we knew as Uncle Bo died as far as I know on the streets of Minneapolis of alcoholism. As a young boy I remember how on occasion there would come a rap at our back door around supper time. It would be Uncle Bo looking for some financial help from my father.

There is another darkness I need to mention as part of my journey and that of our family. This may get a little long but it may also speak to some of you about the darkness in regard to the religion you experience as you make your journey of life. The journey we all are on to find ourselves, to find our God and to find our own wisdom. The darkness was caused by John my older brother who was drafted in the army on April 15, 1953. After boot camp at Fort Leonard Wood, Missouri he without saying anything to us chose to get married to his high school sweetheart Marj Alexander. They were married outside the Catholic Church in Iowa by a Methodist minister on September 25, 1953. At this time in the Catholic Church this would be considered a serious mortal sin. Along with this was the narrow teaching that "outside the Catholic Church there was no salvation." I did not know what teaching my mother carried in her heart from her childhood teaching but John marrying outside the Catholic Church hurt my mother very deeply. Even though she did not share all her feelings I suspect she felt a failure as a Catholic mother, embarrassment in our small town community along with much guilt and many other related feelings.

We tended to focus on our side but also Marj's family being Methodist felt the hurt and rejection of our Catholic teaching. We certainly did not reflect the unconditional love and care of the Risen Cosmic Christ. We did not welcome her into our family. John went on to be a very active Methodist, a loving and responsible husband, father, grandfather and now a great grandfather. He and Marj celebrated their 50th wedding anniversary a few years ago. Since then I was privileged to see how John took such loving care of Marj as she died of a combination of cancer and Alzheimer's disease.

An added indication of the hurt my mother carried came to my awareness only recently when I was visiting John after the wedding of one of his granddaughters. John told me that when Grandma Molitor, mother's mother, had the stroke and died in 1954 mother told John her version of what happened. When a Catholic neighbor told Grandma Molitor about John marrying outside the Catholic Church this was the cause of grandma's stroke and death. So John got the blame for Grandmother Molitor's death. Who knows this for sure but this comment by my mother was very hurtful to my brother and revealed the deep hurt Mother still carried from John's marrying outside the Catholic Church. John and Marj were wonderful to mother all her life and so were their children and grand-children. Yet from different things mother shared with me I felt she never really resolved this issue of John marrying outside the Catholic Church. She took this sadness to her grave. Thank God now in the fullness of the light and love of God she sees and has let go of whatever she was still holding about this darkness in our family. Bishop James Shannon, the then President of the College of St. Thomas, and an excellent teacher made a comment that has stayed with me to this day over 40 years later. His comment was that reeducation was much more difficult than education. In this light, Mother's reeducation never educated her beyond the narrow teachings she learned about Catholics marrying outside of the Catholic Church and its implications for her son John and for herself as his mother.

Bishop Shannon dealt with a different but conscience issue also around the Church's teaching on birth control. This issue amongst other political issues in the church moved him to resign as our local auxiliary Bishop. His resignation as our Bishop was a darkness, a great sadness and surprise to many in the Archdiocese and elsewhere as well.

Another view on John's marriage I need to share is from Marj's side. It was a number of years ago John and Marj and I drove to Iowa to celebrate a funeral of a mutual friend in her Episcopal church. This was Shelly's sister. I knelt next to Marj to share communion together. After communion Marj said she had longed for but never thought she would ever see the day that we knelt together sharing communion in a Christian church. She was so happy. This was her side, which I needed to hear and appreciate as we tend to get focused so many times on our own rather narrow Religious views.

Looking back I am amazed how mother did it, John and Marj did it and we all did it together. As John Henry New-man's poem goes on:

> *Lead Kindly light,*
> *   amid the encircling gloom,*
> *Lead thou me on;*
> *The night is dark and I am far from home.*
> *Lead thou me on.*

The "Kindly Light" of God's love carried my mother and all of us through this darkness.

It was the time in my life journey to move on to my next step in growth. To continue my education these questions surfaced: What to do next? Where to go to school? How to get there? I had in my mind to study business and become a certified public account. I did well in business math and business courses in high school. Where to go? The College of St. Thomas in St. Paul came to my attention and it would be my first experience of Catholic education. Behind this scene, my mother, a dear friend Gert Kiffe who was the junior high principal in the public school, Fr. Nick Walsh a native priest from Farmington, my father's oldest sister Dorothy Caron who looked after her alcoholic brother Uncle Bo, the Benedictine Sisters especially Sister Ignatia and Sister Adelia all were hinting to me at high school graduation time to consider the priesthood.

They felt I had many qualities that would make me a good priest. I was religious and I loved God and I loved people. I enjoyed serving and helping others when in need. I experienced no pressure from any of them but gentle invitations and encouragement. I got their message but I was not ready to accept this call to the Priesthood. I had at the time a lovely Lutheran Girl friend and I looked to get a good job, raise a family and live a comfortable life. So off I went to the College of St. Thomas in St. Paul living off campus. I would come home on weekends to work with my father and be with my family. St. Thomas was only about 30 miles from my home. So this was an easy commute and working on weekends helped me meet the expenses of college.

My graduation from Farmington High School 1952

Me standing by the University of St. Thomas sign - in my day was the College of St. Thomas

CHAPTER THREE

Off To College Of St. Thomas 1952-1953

*"I fled Him, down the nights and down the days;
I fled Him, down the arches of the years; I fled Him,
down the labyrinthine ways of my own mind;
and in the midst of tears I hid from Him,
and under running laughter."*

"The Hound of Heaven" by Francis Thompson

15

I chose to attend St. Thomas College, my first experience in Catholic School. What to study was the question before I left high school. Studying for a CPA seemed a direction in which to go. I chose classes to meet this business major.

I quote above "The Hound of Heaven" since God as the "Hound of Heaven" kept after me about becoming a priest.

I expected Religion classes to be interesting. I found they were not challenging, in fact boring. English with Dr. James Colwell was the most interesting and challenging class of my freshman year. His introduction of T. S. Eliot awakened me to more spiritual values; if I recall accurately it was his poem, "The Hollow Men" among others.

Those who have crossed

With direct eyes,
*   to death's other kingdom*

Remember us—if at all—
*   not as lost*

Violent souls, but only

As the hollow men

The stuffed men.

"The Hollow Men" by T.S. Eliot

My term paper choice for the class was the Atomic bombing of Hiroshima. This raised my consciousness and touched my heart as to the tragedy and destruction of war. It posed the question to my heart that maybe as a priest I could be an effective channel of peace. The memory of this term paper was still with me when at St. Matthew's I spoke out from the pulpit against the Vietnam War. Now as I write, we are destroying the most ancient culture in the world with our war in Iraq and Afghanistan. We are creating thousand of refugees and widows and orphans. Many of our beloved soldiers are wounded or dead.

"The Hound of Heaven" kept chasing after me to decide what I wanted to do with my life. I spent many days on my knees praying in the college chapel. Seeking guidance and enlightenment, the Hound of Heaven was whispering in the ear of my heart to follow God's call to be a priest. This call did not appeal to me. It, to my mind and heart, called me to give up the many aspects of life I loved and enjoyed. Yet if I was to be faithful to myself and my God, the response had to be yes.

I discussed this with Father Fredric Bieter at St. Thomas – the advisor of the young men studying at St. Thomas who were interested in becoming priests. He suggested to me that I could stay on at St. Thomas or go to Nazareth Hall, the minor seminary. I also discussed this with Father Bill Baumgaertner, my logic professor, who was also on the faculty at St. Paul Seminary. With their guidance and listening to the "hound of heaven" speaking to my heart, it seemed best for me to go to Nazareth Hall. Familiar and comfortable distractions would be removed, allowing me to focus more clearly on my possible vocation to the priesthood. Financially the choice for Nazareth Hall would fit my limitation of funds for college.

So off I went to Nazareth Hall. This opened another step on my life journey and a very challenging one. This decision created a real stretch for my mother to balance the opposites and develop her *Aware Ego*. Her oldest son had married outside the Church and was no longer active in the Catholic Church. Her second oldest son was choosing to become a priest in the Church, making him very active in the Church. I would say mother held in her heart very quietly and with mixed emotions the tension of these opposites.

1955 Graduation class from Nazareth Hall -
I am in the middle of the front row.

CHAPTER FOUR

Back To High School
Nazareth Hall
1953-1955

Why back to high school? After my freshman year in college at St. Thomas, going now to the minor seminary was like going back to high school. Nazareth Hall was a boarding four-year high school and two-year college. It was located in a beautiful setting on Lake Johanna north of St. Paul. There were about 180 students total. I made up my mind to meet this challenge but under this brave front I was scared and vulnerable.

It was difficult entering into this new life experience. I had made the decision to honor the "Hound of Heaven" and say, "yes" to the call to be a priest. My first roommate Art Shields, a graduate of Cretin High School, was brilliant and gifted in many ways. To my surprise he left in the middle of the first year. I do not know for sure why he left, and his early departure left me feeling unsure about my own commitment. The rector Father Louis McCarthy and the spiritual director Father Ambrose Hayden were my two significant mentors at the time. I shared my concerns and fears with them. With their help and encouragement, along with study and prayer, I remained faithful to my initial decision. My initial connection with Father McCarthy and Father Hayden has been an ongoing support along my journey whenever I needed their wisdom and help.

Few of the seminarians were public school graduates as I was. Lacking language background except English from my high school meant staying on an extra year at Nazareth Hall to learn Latin that was scarcely used or ever going to be used. With this extra year and limited choices of other classes, I took on first-year Greek. Languages were difficult for me, but I persevered, doing well. Actually studying Greek as well as Latin helped me understand better our English language.

I was introduced to ice hockey. Many of the students played well, long, and hard. I managed to fit in and I actually enjoyed the game. I needed the exercise and fresh air and hockey as a winter sport fit the bill. Basketball was more the inside winter sport. I played B team basketball back at home in Farmington – I did about the same at the minor seminary.

Father Dick Moudry was our English professor. He introduced our class to John Henry Cardinal Newman by studying Newman's classic *Apologia Pro Vita Sua*. Father Dick engendered in me a love for Cardinal Newman. I was impressed with Newman's complete candor, his shining honesty, his fidelity to God and to truth. This was the beginning of Cardinal Newman becoming one of my significant mentors even up to this day.

After being accustomed to the public school environment and its free-dom, the schedule of the minor seminary was very structured. The Ger-man Franciscan Sisters of St. Paul fed us well and took loving care of us when we were sick. In a way, they were our mothers away from home. They filled the role well. In spite of their love and care, I did become dis-couraged and lonely at times. I questioned if this being a priest was for me. I consulted Father Hayden and Fr. McCarthy. I prayed often and I hung in there.

During this time my grandmother on my mother's side died. She was very dear to me. We lived with her for many years after my grandfather died. She and my grandfather were devout Catholics and close to the church. They in turn raised my mother and her sister Charlotte as devout Catholics. I remember well when I told my grandmother I was going to study to become a priest. Her reaction surprised me. I thought she would be excited and happy for my choice. But she was not and to this day I re-gret I did not ask her why.

While I was studying at Nazareth Hall, she had a stroke and died in our local hospital. I did have a visit with her before she died. Her passing was a big loss for me. We were what I would call "close buddies." I remember enjoying walking to church with her many Sundays. We also were an ex-cellent team working together on keeping up the lawn and other chores around the house. I was always happy to find her at home when I came home from school. She always had jobs for me to do.

She never expressed this feeling to me, but I felt that after the stroke she did not want to become a burden to our family. Grandma experienced taking care of my grandfather before he died of cancer. My sense was she decided to surrender, go home to heaven to be with her God, her hus-band, two of her children that died at birth, and many other family and friends who had gone before her.

I finished my two years at Nazareth Hall. The extra year was for com-pleting my studies with Latin. This extra year made me part of two dif-ferent classes in the Seminary. With relief, some fear and apprehension and with much joy and gratitude in my heart I went on to the next leg of my life journey. This was to the St. Paul Seminary. The Seminary that was just across the street from St. Thomas College where I had attended two years ago as a freshman. The curriculum at the Major Seminary would be two years of Philosophy and four years of Theology.

Feb. 19, 1961 - My ordination celebration at the St. Paul Cathedral

CHAPTER FIVE

St. Paul Seminary
1955-1961

"Life is a journey to find ourselves,

To find our God and to find our own wisdom."

T he St. Paul Seminary was my next step to the priesthood and more importantly the next step on my journey to finding myself, my God and my own wisdom.

The aula maxima where most of our classes were held was a large lecture hall. As in most colleges and universities where the classes are large, they tended to be boring. A maxim floating around the campus, which made sense to me in this context, was: "Do not let your classes interfere with your education."

For me this meant, in addition to regular class work, the reading of Teihard de Chardin, John Henry Newman, Bede Griffith, the Gospels, The Epistles of St. Paul, Ghandi, Dorothy Day, Baroness Catherine de Hueck, founder of Friendship House, Carl Jung and many others. To this day these and others have been important mentors in guiding me on my life journey. With Jim Barry a classmate and friend from the New Ulm diocese we found a common mentor in Dorothy Day.

The church was moving into Vatican II and not all our classes prepared us for this change in the energy of the Church. These mentors kept me in tune with the energy and spirit of Vatican II and our modern world. When I think of Ghandi I think of his words of wisdom, which fit so well with our present national and international economic situation. "For the Greedy there is never enough. For the Needy there is always enough." My take is the Greedy never even see the Needy.

My spiritual director for some of my time at the Seminary was Father Bill Baumgaertner who was on the Philosophy Faculty in the Seminary. He had been my logic teacher when I was a freshman at St. Thomas College. He suggested that I might want to choose one mentor and read more about him and have him as a friend on my life journey. The mentor I chose was my friend from Father Dick Moudry's English class at Nazareth Hall, John Henry

Studying hard at my desk at the St. Paul Seminary

Cardinal Newman. This choice has provided a wonderful support per-

24

son in my life when the road on the journey was rough, discouraging and pretty dark at times.

I have read and reread his letters, his sermons and his many biographies along with rereading his *Apologia Pro Vita Sua*. Newman loved God, his family, his friends and the truth. His complete candor, his shining honesty, his love for the truth at whatever personal cost to himself lead him into the Roman Catholic Church. As I mentioned earlier about the consciousness process of the *Aware Ego*, the *Aware Ego* was very much alive and growing in his life.

I see Newman had an *Aware Ego* in many areas of opposites in his life. He understood well and embraced the opposites of tradition and modern thought. He embraced the spirit of Vatican I and Vatican II even before it took place. He was an extremely brilliant and gifted teacher and preacher but did not seek the lime light. Rather give up and get discouraged in very difficult attacks on even his personal integrity he showed courage and humility and fidelity to his Kindly Light. He was a person of deep personal prayer and also of action. He held the tension between the Church of England and the Roman Catholic Church and made the very difficult choice to join the Roman Catholic Church. With this decision he lost his friends in the Church of England. He was forbidden to return to his beloved Oxford. To top this off he was not accepted with open arms by the Roman Catholic Hierarchy who seemed to fear him at the time. He was not welcomed and respected in the way he deserved. Yet he humbly went his way being faithful to the Kindly Light of God and his own conscience.

Friends, as for Cardinal Newman, are a significant part of our lives. This was and is true for me. The most joy of my seminary days was the friends I met. Many of them are still part of my life. Some have died and many have since left the active priesthood. I am not exactly sure of this but out of our class of 50 which included priests from other dioceses studying with us, about half are alive and still in active ministry.

Coming out of a public school background both in grade school and high school left me somewhat on the outside. Most of my classmates were products of Catholic grade schools, high schools, colleges and seminaries. This feeling of being left out was not enough to discourage me in any way. I may not have had as good an education as I may have gotten from a private Catholic school. My more open experience of life in the public schools and my mixing with a wide variety of young people, teachers and dating all provided richness in my education in a different way. I experienced this as a plus in my life journey.

Being a person of prayer was an important value in my seminary life as it is now. Prayer, as for Cardinal Newman, has carried me along on my life journey through many a storm. Some form of daily meditation seemed necessary for my stability and spiritual growth. Over the years I had experimented with many forms of meditation. For about the last fifteen years or so my two mentors or I should say three in Meditation practice are John Main whose work is continued by his successor Laurence Freeman, Thich Nhat Hanh the world renowned Vietnamese Zen master, teacher and author and Bede Griffiths. I like Bede's description of Contemplation: "Seeing and Hearing with the Heart." John Main says it in this way," Being present to God who is always present to us and is Presence."

John Main's teaching which is very similar to the others is: Relax and find a silent place; keep your back straight to keep you awake and the energy circulating up and down your spine; gently close your eyes and for twenty to thirty minutes repeat a mantra and if possible join this with following your breath. Distractions will come and when they do gently go back to your mantra and your breath. John recommends practicing this discipline twice a day. If you are interested and for more detail go to his teachings and to the others I mentioned. Meditation simply is a discipline to keep us mindful or living in the present moment where life is, where God is, where grace and recovery is.

Peter Oh from Korea and Rudy Pruden an African American were the only non-Caucasian students on campus. For some reason they became special friends of mine during these years. Rudy never finished Seminary study and was never ordained a priest. We still keep in contact. Peter was ordained in our Cathedral with our class and then went back to Korea to be groomed to be the local native Bishop. He experienced extreme stress caused by his workload back in the Chancery in Korea. Another cause of stress was that some fellow priests were making political moves against him. It might have been that they were jealous of his study opportunities leading to his being the first native Bishop. These stresses took their toll on his health forcing him to resign from active ministry. He married a lovely Korean Nurse. Many of his family live in the States and he came here to work in the office of his Sister and Brother-in-law, both talented doctors in the Chicago area. We are still friends and he lives in the Chicago area where I have visited him. It was my plan someday to visit Korea. His Episcopal Ordination of Bishop would be that occasion. He never became Bishop and I have never gone to Korea.

My father died of a heart attack in my second year at the Seminary. He died suddenly on December 23 while buying gas at the local Mobil station. The station was just across the street from Shelly Inc. where we both worked. We waked him at home as was the custom – clearing out from our living room the Christmas tree and other decorations to make room for his casket. I was touched with all the support and presence of the students and the faculty of the Seminary along with so many relatives and friends in Farmington. Shelly, my father's boss as well as friend touched my heart in not being afraid to show his sadness and love for my father by crying. I never realized how much Shelly respected and loved my father. When my only sister got married I took my father's place walking her down the aisle.

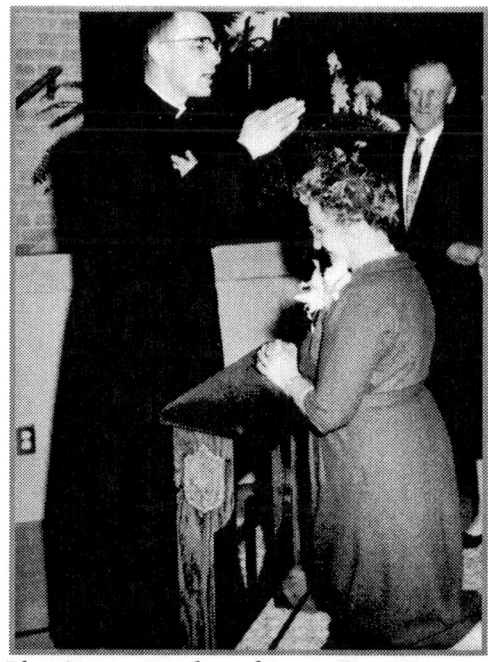

Some days were long and then as happens the years go by and one day I found myself standing at the altar of the Cathedral in St. Paul. I am ordained a priest. My first Mass was at St. Michael's Catholic Church in Farmington, my home parish. From there I would move on to minister in our local Archdiocesan Church.

Blessing my mother after my First Mass at St. Michael's Church in Farmington

There is one memory that I find embarrassing to mention. I was home for Christmas after being ordained a deacon. I was given the privilege to preach at all the Christmas Masses. I seem to recall I preached far too long. My pastor and the parishioners were kind to this newly ordained deacon. It seems to me I should have gotten the message as parishioners were dozing off right in front of my nose. My best move would have been to scrap the long written homily. After that just share from my heart my joy in celebrating with them the Incarnation of Jesus Christ this Christmas. I had not learned yet what Cardinal Newman meant by speaking from Heart to Heart. I was a slow learner then. Still am in many ways today.

Here I am the newly ordained priest

Church of the Maternity of Mary

CHAPTER SIX

Church of Maternity of Mary
1961-1965

A Journey Of Thousand Miles
Begins With A Single Step.

The first step in my journey as a priest was being the associate pastor at the Church of Maternity of Mary in St. Paul, Minnesota. On my day of arrival the building of the new parish church was underway. New ground was being broken not only for the church building but also for my ministry. Ironically to the pastor the building of a new church and money were more important than my ministry and the building of the community of the people.

Almost from the first day there, I was welcomed and hit in the face with the remark of the pastor who told me he did not want me. He only needed me for Sunday Masses. This was my welcome and I was tolerated. This set the tone of my initial ministry as a young priest.

This assignment was considered one of the most difficult in the Archdiocese. Many of my classmates also had similar assignments with difficult pastors. As young priests we were excited by the new life of the Spirit of Vatican II. Most of the Pastors lived in the spirit of Vatican I and tolerated the Spirit of Vatican II. Life was not easy both for us and for them in this transition time of renewal in the Catholic Church.

I loved the people at Maternity of Mary and they loved me. I did much work with the youth. One mother of a large and dedicated family fell in love with me. I gave her attention and a feeling response that she did not get from her husband. She was open with me and I with her. Her love for me did not get acted out and was honored by both of us. This falling in love with parishioners and vice versa happens to all of us and happened to me a number of times on my life journey. It shows we are all human and men and women. It seems to me we need to own these experiences, deal with them openly and honestly and not act them out with affairs and the like. This applies to married couples as they experience similar fallings in love with other than their spouse or partner.

One of my first celebrations of Confirmation in the parish brought me into contact with a lovely family who helped keep me healthy and alive. We are friends to this day, forty-five years later. I was standing outside after the confirmation celebration. Roger Ayde, a Lutheran and father of one of the young men confirmed, saw me standing there alone. Roger suggested to his son and wife that I be invited to

Roger and Margaret Ayde celebrating their 25th Wedding Anniversary

their home for an after confirmation party. Roger as a Lutheran, the husband and father in a mixed marriage, was not well accepted by the pastor. Roger was big enough and generous enough to contend with this and seemingly did not let it bother him.

From that day on I spent many Sundays at their lake cabin learning to water ski, enjoying swimming, sailing and playing volleyball. I so enjoyed the energy of their family and their many friends who also had sons and daughters in the parish. I, in one sense, see them and especially Roger with his generous and open spirit, the savior of my life and vocation in this difficult first assignment. This was another Aware Ego opposite for me to embrace and live with its tension. There was the spirit of the more conservative and rigid Vatican I pastor and the opposite in the open and spirit filled joy of the Ayde's and their friends enjoying life and freedom at their lake cabin.

They say your first assignment sets you into many habits for life. The pastor was rigid about lighting in the church. The lights were not turned on until people could barely see to read their missals. Apparently it was important to save money on the electric bill. This brought about complaining as well as laughter. Forty-five years later I am frugal in turning off unnecessary lights in the church or on in my residence. I got the habit.

As one of my duties I wrote the parish bulletin and the pastor would edit it. Most of the time what I wrote remained as I had written it. I remember with hurt and disappointment, and with no big surprise, the final censure the pastor made in the last bulletin I prepared. I wrote a farewell and thank you to the parish. I quoted the sermon theme from John Henry Newman's "Parting of Friends." This was the quote from Newman in his more classical 19th century English:

"O, my brethren, O kind and affectionate hearts, O loving friends, should you know anyone whose lot is has been, by writing or by word of mouth, in some degree to help you thus to act: If he has ever told you what you knew about yourselves or what you did not know; has read to you your wants or feelings, and comforted you by the very reading; has made you feel that there was a higher life than this daily one and a brighter world than that you see; or encouraged you, or sobered you, or opened a way to the inquiring, or soothed the perplexed; if what he has said or done has ever made you take interest in him and feel well inclined towards him; remember such a one in time to come, though you hear him not, pray for him, that in all things he may know God's will, and at all times he may be ready to fulfill it."

When the bulletin came out my farewell and thank you had been excluded. Knowing the spirit of the pastor, this did not surprise me. The fact that there was no parish farewell reception for me did not surprise me either. I need to be honest though and admit it hurt me inside. I also felt sorry for the Pastor whose heart functioned in this manner. There were farewells but only the ones in private homes of those who loved me and would miss me.

I served four years in this assignment. This was the longest any associate had worked with this pastor. I do not know whether my choosing to stay on for four years in this difficult assignment was a complement or insult to me. For the sake of my vocation and the quality of my life and health, I had to move on. Father Louis McCarthy from my Nazareth Hall days who was now a Monsignor helped me again. He was instrumental in having me reassigned.

This had not been a healthy beginning for my first step in my journey of the priesthood. I did persevere and by God's Generous Grace I am still in active ministry 49 years later. My mentor John Henry Cardinal Newman was a model and strength for me. His treatment by the Church when he entered was far worse. He endured and persisted amazingly so in his vocation with humility and no resentments.

Life goes on. My ministry and journey as a priest goes on.

Church of St. Matthew

CHAPTER SEVEN

Church of St. Matthew
1965-1971

From The Frying Pan Into The Fire

I left with joy, relief, and some sadness "the frying pan" of the Church of Maternity Mary. I moved on with excitement to a new experience at the Church of St. Matthew, an old German national parish on the west side of St. Paul. The pastor sets the tone of the parish and this was quite a contrast of opposites for me—a conservative and controlling administrative type of pastor at Maternity of Mary to a retired teacher, non-administrative type at St. Matthew's.

God is good. I was blessed to have a young associate to share ministry with me. We helped each other deal with the challenges of the parish and helped each other grow. He was Don Wegscheider, newly ordained, a gifted artist, and a great people person. Together, we made a wonderful pastoral team. At this time we both came down off the clerical pedestal and became human. At the same time we owned with appropriate professional dignity the opposite that we were priests of God.

Our rectory was a very large old home which had combined a couple of houses into one large rectory. There were suites of rooms each for Don, for me, the Pastor, our live-in housekeeper Mary, and a couple guest rooms for visiting weekend priests. This big old wooden rectory was directly across the street from the church. I love big old houses and I loved this one. Since we had the room, a young priest who we both knew (older than Don and younger than I) asked if he could stay with us. He was struggling with depression and searching for his identity separate from being a priest. He was very bright and a student of Carl Jung. He piqued my interest in the work of Carl Jung. I was, like so many priests, searching for my identity and even questioning my commitment to priesthood. The teaching of Carl Jung was a help in this journey of searching for our identities. Interest in Carl Jung took me to a Jungian conference in Texas, where I met Hal Stone, a Jungian analyst from Los Angeles. Hal was moving along with a broader avenue for his own personal and professional life in the area of Holistic Health and Healing. He later established the Center for Healing Arts in West Los Angeles. I would say the Center, in exploring the holistic way to view disease and health, was the first of its kind in the country and maybe the world. This area of interest was mine as well, so I got on his mailing list. Guess what? This interest set off in me a new fire for life and growth.

On Easter Monday there was a fire that set our community on fire with new life and growth. This was an actual fire that literally burned out the old brick German church. It had to be demolished.

At the time of the fire the Pastor was in Minneapolis visiting the library as he often did and Don was off on a short post-Easter holiday. I was home alone. It was chaos around the church with fire sirens and fire engines all over the place. The Firemen tried to save what they could from the church and of the church. Parishioners and other spectators were watching with sadness and fear and many with camera in hand. When things settled down I was not quite sure how to let the pastor know what happened. He often got home after I was asleep. What to do to let him know? We often left notes for each other as a form of communication. I was feeling awkward on this occasion about leaving a note, but what else could I do, with no cell phones at this time. I left him a note that our parish church burned. If he was watching the news where he was visiting, he would have heard about it. So this was the literal fire after the frying pan of Maternity Mary. As you might suspect the symbolic fire was just beginning to burn, bringing death but also new life.

The fire created a challenge for me that made this part of my life journey a new and very difficult experience. The pastor was not a good administrator. He could not have organized the resources to build a new church. So I was appointed administrator by the Archbishop's office to head up the building of the new church. To save face for the pastor and get things, done my appointment was not made public. No one else knew what my role was, so many in the parish thought I was taking over where the pastor should be in charge. A charge he was not able to meet.

I took charge and it was not easy. There was lots of gossip about my taking over. Who was I to be doing this, not respecting the pastor? I was aware before the fire of many of the mismanagement issues to be dealt with. But now as Administrator I discovered many more issues that had to be settled. Besides the building of a new church, the finances were not in good order. Bills were not paid, and mail had not been opened or checks cashed for years. Mass stipends that were not honored were in the hundreds. At this point I made a decision not to consult the pastor on any of these matters, because if I did nothing would have gotten done. Looking back I suspect in many ways he was happy I chose to operate this way. The appointment made it clear I was in charge. But still this was not easy to balance these opposites, live in the same house and eat at the same table.

Along with our local fire there were many other fires happening in our world at this time. These required balance of opposites. They affected my life and the life of the parish community. This was the time of the Viet Nam war and all the controversy around our involvement in it. I spoke out against our involvement in the war. My term paper back at St. Thomas on the Atomic Bombing of Hiroshima was still in my consciousness about the tragedy and uselessness of war. My speaking about the Commandment "thou shall not kill" (as you might suspect) got me in some hot water with the supporters of the war. There was the tension of opposites in the Catholic Church as Vatican II moved the Church into a new area of life and growth, set on fire by the Holy Spirit. The Cursillo movement and Charismatic movement were setting off the fire of love in the Church and creating a tension of opposites. Again the question was how to keep a balance in the parish communities and in the lives of priests, religious women and men, and lay people. The Civil rights movement was strong. This was the time of Martin Luther King and the Berrigan brothers. Along with all this our Archdiocese was shocked by the resignation of Bishop James Shannon who was caught in these same challenges and tensions of opposites. Bishop Shannon was well loved and respected, a mentor and ideal of many priests and lay people in the archdiocese, including myself.

In the first chapter I mentioned that an *Aware Ego* is able to hold the tension of the opposites. Looking back now I sense I had an *Aware Ego* in progress at this time in my ministry and did not know it. My *Aware Ego* carried me through so much necessary tension and the balancing of opposites. It kept me grounded, focused and connected to my deeper self and my God amidst all the tension of these opposites.

Emotions were expressed in sadness, confusion, and anger over the destruction of the historical German church. The old church held many family memories for the long-time parishioners. Confusion was equally high regarding who was in charge of the parish, since the matter of my appointment was not public. I hired Bea Groetsch as a secretary to help me sort out all the administrative confusion. Bill Wolf a retired banker came in to help sort out much of the money issues. What do we do with all the dated and uncashed checks? Bea and Bill helped me with their skills to get the job done, and done well with appropriate confidentiality. We enabled each other to keep the balance by humor and generosity and not taking ourselves too seriously.

The remains of Old St. Matthew's Church

Ever since then Bill and Bea have been dear friends of mine. Bill has gone home to heaven to be with his lovely wife. Bea is ready and waiting to be called home to be with her beloved husband Howard and son Jerry.

The challenge was not an easy one to hold the tension of the opposites. I needed to do what was necessary to serve the parish and our God. A parish council and finance committee were needed to help me guide the parish. A building committee was needed to move on the construction of a new church. To function well I needed to share with these people my appointment as administrator. This involvement of the lay parishioners was a new phenomenon for this community and created talk, jealousy, misunderstanding, and other mixed emotions in the parish community. But it set an ongoing fire under this German community. Fire brings energy, new life, and excitement along with the destruction of the old. I, with lots of dedicated help, was called to hold the balance in all this chaos around death and new life. The *Aware Ego* appears again.

A key question was: What kind of church do you build? It was not practical to try to duplicate the old German church. Building a Church is highly emotional, and there is no way you could please everyone. Luckily the insurance agent was a parishioner who made sure the insurance policy was up to date. Our funds were limited and the site of the new church was limited to the site of the old church. The old neighboring church of St. Michael the Irish national church was available. We used that and our school gym for Sunday Masses during construction time.

82-Year-Old Church Building Gives Way To New, Modern Structure . . .

I find it interesting and fascinating how God works in our lives. I was involved in the building of the new church at Maternity Mary, never suspecting I would be involved in building another new church. We even ended up having the same architect that we had at Maternity.

After much work, discussion, and many meetings a more contemporary church was built. We installed chairs instead of pews and kneelers. This would aid the elderly and many others in moving more freely in and out of the seating. Bill Wolf came up with this practical suggestion. People were invited to stand instead of kneel and there were lots of objections to this. But most people were not aware that the big churches and cathedrals in Europe and in Rome do not have kneelers and many have no pews. A few statues were included as recommended by the Instruction on the Liturgy as well as a separate Blessed Sacrament Chapel. The chapel as a sacred space would house the Eucharist and be a suitable space for private prayer. This would be something like the Holy of Holies in the Jewish Temple. The church space was organized to be open, and could be used for concerts, plays, musicals and lectures, and other educational functions for adults or for the school.

When the church was completed, a grand opening took place with parishioners marching with banners and music from all four directions of the community. We were celebrating and saying Thank you to our God for the new life that had come from the fire.

After all this I was amazed I was still alive and smiling but I was. It must have been my *Aware Ego* keeping the balance and connecting me to myself and my God. Along with this were the support and a wonderful sense of humor of those working closely with me. We did not take ourselves too seriously and could see the humorous side of many things that were not so humorous.

The pastor moved to a retirement home in Minneapolis. Again to save face, we both were moved at the same time. I personally would have liked to stay on for a few more years to enjoy our fired up community and the new church building, but this was not to be. In another sense I was ready to move on and shake the accumulated dust from my feet. I went on to be officially and publicly appointed pastor of the Church of St. Pius X in White Bear Lake. The title of John Henry Newman's sermon "The Second Spring" fits this situation. I used a short quotation for a bulletin reflection.

> "We mourn over the blossoms of May, because they are to wither; but we know, withal, that May is one day to have its revenge upon November, by revolution of that solemn circle which never stops, which teaches us in our height of hope, ever to be sober, and in our depth of desolation never to despair."

The Church of St. Matthew experienced a second spring.

Often over the years different pastors and others asked me how I got so much new life and activity, a second spring, at St. Matthew's. My response: "Start a fire."

My traveling companion at St. Matthew's

St. Pius X Church

CHAPTER EIGHT

Church of St. Pius X
1971-1978

Change Is A Process, Not An Event

As I chose this quotation to begin this next chapter, it brought to mind Hal and Sidra Stone's description of the *Aware Ego* as not a thing but a process. So the process of my life journey moved me from the old west side German community to the new young suburban church of St. Pius X in White Bear Lake. Again these communities were opposites in so many ways so tension, and also balance, was called for.

Two Priest Friends then and now- left Roger Pierre, center Jerry Kern, right me

Before I left St. Matthew's I had planned a needed Education experience and Holiday with a priest friend Father Jerry Kern. All arrangements were made to attend a Bernard Lonergan Conference at Milltown in Dublin. We then would travel around Ireland. This was my first visit to Ireland, but I think Jerry had been there once before. The Archdiocese surprised me by assigning me to St. Pius X at this time. All the plans for Ireland were made. We were not going to change them. I needed the break, so we went. Jerry was familiar with Lonergan, since he studied under him in Rome. He was excited to study under Lonergan again and he recommended this Conference for me. I learned much and did enjoy Lonergan. One thing that has stuck with me to this day was Lonergan's teaching about Romans 5 as the essence of the Christian message and life. "God's love poured forth in our hearts by the Holy Spirit." Even today I feel this message is not fully acknowledged and lived out. Bernard Lonergan is a very gifted and brilliant Theologian and I wished I had more opportunities to study under him. My sense the Church needs to be more in tune and attentive to his Theological Wisdom.

God also came along at this time. God provided John Riehle, a gifted musician and educated deacon, to be part of my staff. I knew John and his family from St. Matthew's. His father Fred was very active in helping us

42

bring new life to the community of St. Matthew's after the fire. John stepped in and helped the transition of my coming as the new pastor. Since I came the first Sunday but needed to leave for the Conference that week John was a real God send and filled in well. John stayed on as a respected staff member even after I left as Pastor.

Since again the Pastor sets the tone or energy of the parish community, St. Pius X was very different from the older German community of St. Matthew. My predecessor was into control and hands-on administration and these were his forte. This was my first parish assignment as pastor. My previous experience in the other parishes helped me meet this challenge. To my surprise this community was more conservative than the community of St. Matthew, especially after the fire called it to new life.

The challenge for me was to adjust backward, being careful not to compare Parish communities. I had a tendency to compare to encourage growth and new life. Not so smart. In moving from one parish to another you oftentimes inherit the staff of the previous pastor. This can be both a plus and a minus. In this case I inherited the previous pastor's secretary, who was dying of cancer. This was not an easy challenge. We met it and took good care of her.

As in most parishes there was a group around the previous pastor who he controlled, and also in a sense controlled him. My challenge was to break through this and make the inner circle more inclusive of the total parish. This was not so easy and again I found the tension of opposites.

I remember about this time as my leadership was becoming more inclusive Father Roger Pierre approached me to join me in ministry as an associate pastor. An associate was definitely needed. He asked me how things were going with the settling of the dust that always arises with a new pastor coming in. I assured him things were going well. I encouraged him to come on in and join me. The day he arrived the news broke that a group of parishioners not open to a more inclusive involvement had worked out with a Religious priest living in the parish community to make St. Pius X a Religious Parish. If this happened it would move me out as a Diocesan Priest. A Pastor would be appointed from the Religious Community. This was my welcome to Father Roger. Together we weathered this storm, and the parish did not become a Religious Parish. Roger and I had many complementary gifts, so this worked well for us and the community in holding the tension of opposites. I thank God to this day for this gift of Roger and the Parish Community. We all grew spiritually. I have always appreciated and needed having another priest in the house to share life, decisions, frustrations, and ministry concerns. Roger provided this well for me and I provided the same for him.

Another tension of opposites in all the three parishes I had so far been involved in concerned parish school parents and families, and those parents and families not involved in the school. The challenge and tension was how to balance the budget to make sure all the money did not go for the school. The other religious programs needed to receive their share in the budget.

We struggled to balance the opposites and make the tension livable. Part of the challenge for me was that I never attended a Catholic Grade School or High School, so I did not have the same focus of energy just for the school which was pretty common in most parishes with schools. We added staff to enhance and develop further the religious education programs for children and adults both in the school and in other Religious education programs. We also worked with the school staff. This helped bring about the balance needed. There was still some tension as there always is in holding these opposites.

Another challenge was the selling of the convent building which was not needed any more for housing the Religious Sisters. Different offers came in for halfway houses of one kind or another. We kept the neighbors informed, because they wanted and needed to be informed.

Most offers by halfway houses of some kind were feared and not acceptable by the neighbors. Again God stepped in. The Franciscan Sisters of Little Falls were looking for a House of Prayer. Our convent fit their bill so they moved in and were a wonderful addition to our parish community. This provided an added gift to me by making some wonderful friends of many of the Sisters. Sister Thomasine, until the day God called her home a few years back, had been a wonderful friend and support of me and my Fr. Gulliver adventures.

At this time in my life journey I was very conscious of the role of women in the church and their lack of power and significant involvement. I think St. Pius X was the first parish in the Archdiocese to have a woman as President of the Parish Council. Some women felt the call to be a priest which I was open to. The Church was not open to women priests, so many women just left the Church feeling left out by the Church. One Sunday I had prepared a homily on the role of women in the Church and questioned why they were excluded from priesthood. Just before I gave the homily it dawned on me the laity in the parish might agree or disagree with me, but they had no power to do anything about the situation of women in the Church. Thinking Archbishop Roach would be more likely to be able to do something about this issue, I made a taped copy of my homily and sent it on to him. I did not hear back from him and did not expect to. But also I realized, knowing the politics of the Church, Archbishop Roach could not really speak out on the issue. Even though I felt he was very supportive of women's involvement in the Church.

This reflection brings to mind a very recent discussion with my first cousin Nancy Whittier Akin, who was married to a classmate of mine Pat Akin, and one of the few of my relatives still living in Farmington. When Nancy married Pat she became a Catholic and a very good one hanging in there when many others might have left. Nancy nursed Pat through a journey of living with Parkinson's and she is now a widow. She has genetic connections for the disease of alcoholism on both sides of her family. One of her gifted sons is still caught in the claws of alcoholism and her twin brother died of alcoholism. Besides this, through a nerve mishap of some kind, Nancy had to have her leg amputated so she lives with a prosthesis. Nancy very faithfully goes to Saturday evening Mass at St. Michael's and she provides a ride for two of her neighbors. One of these neighbors is a lovely devout Catholic woman, who has a daughter who felt called to be a priest. Since the Catholic Church was not open to this, the daughter joined another Christian Church that allowed her to be a priest/minister and she is happy there. Her mother is not happy, but sad. But the Church could just say "let her go" or provide for women to be ordained in the Catholic Church. I would prefer the latter. Along with this Nancy and Pat's children belong to other Christian Churches, not the Catholic Church. When Pat died the local pastor could not be reached. I was called and was happy to preside. But also her Lutheran children said, if dad cannot be buried in the Catholic Church, he is welcome to be buried in our Lutheran Church. So the challenges of the Institutional Catholic Church go on for better or for worse.

The fire of consciousness set alive with Hal Stone and the Center for the Healing Arts was kept burning by my being involved in an annual summer conference sponsored by the Center. Hal was always supportive of me with tuition breaks and helps with housing. I had a fascinating dream at my first conference. Hal's dear friend, who I was staying with, suggested I spend the night with Hal. That night I had the dream that I remained a priest following Hal. The other priest classmate left ministry and went his own way. I am still as it were following Hal and still a priest, and my life and priesthood have been enriched immensely. The classmate in the dream did leave active ministry.

With the interest of many parishioners a healing group was started in the parish. The Group was one of choice. They met regularly to discuss what I had learned at the summer conferences. Besides education and discussion we sent healing energy to those who needed it including ourselves. Over thirty years later I am still indebted to and am friends with these members. We learned together and they challenged me and supported me in my interest when at this time holistic health and healing was considered way out and not mainstream as much as it is today.

Also at this time I was introduced to Hazelden, the treatment and training center for persons living with addictions. A priest from Kentucky trained there and lived with me in White Bear Lake. He introduced me to a Parish Based Clinical Pastoral Education Program provided by Hazelden. As I had made the decision to move on to a new assignment, I used the Parish Based Clinical Pastoral Education program to look at my leaving the parish. I wanted to take care of the best I could all my needs and those of the parish as I moved on. I learned much from this program. It helped me take care of myself as I left St. Pius X. It also helped me to take care of St. Pius X parish in a suitable manner. At Hazelden I also learned how Hazelden's treatment of their clients included the spirituality of the 12 Steps of AA. Besides this Hazelden, with their Minnesota model of recovery, followed the holistic model of healing very similar to what I was learning about from Hal at the Center for the Healing Arts. What resulted from all this was my leaving St. Pius X to take a sabbatical. My sabbatical was to study for a year with Hal at the Center for the Healing Arts in West Los Angeles. This is another chapter in my life journey to find myself, my own wisdom, and to find my God.

Church of St. Mary Magdalen

CHAPTER NINE

Church of St. Mary Magdalen
1978-1979

If Nothing Changes, Nothing Changes.

I needed a change from the pressure of parish life, so I made a change. I was bold and trusting in taking a sabbatical when they were not a part of the policy in the Archdiocese. Here again Monsignor Hayden behind the scenes took care so that my Health insurance would not be discontinued during this year away.

I made arrangements with Hal Stone to study for the next year at the Center for the Healing Arts in West Los Angeles. How to get there and where to live were my basic questions. I wrote to the Chancery office in Los Angeles about a parish I might live in for this year. In exchange for helping with duties at the parish I could get room and board. Father Sullivan the pastor in a small parish in West Los Angeles wrote me. He understood the situation and knew that the possibilities for a suitable parish were not too good. In his generosity he offered me hospitality at the Church of St. Mary Magdalen in West Los Angeles. What a gift that was; I never realized it at the time. Father Sullivan was about my age, with some health issues, and was a Chicago priest gone west. He was what I would consider conservative, but generous and easy going. God again took good care of me by providing this opportunity for a place to stay. The Church of St. Mary Magdalen was very close to the Center for the Healing Arts. As I look back now I had a very high trust level and God did take extremely good care of me.

Laura and Peter (good friends of mine from St. Matthew's) and I drove two cars to Los Angeles. We camped along the way. I cannot imagine doing this now but did it then. I drove my little five-speed Capri and they drove in Peter's car. We kept together, camped together and got along well in spite of all our differences. This was in 1978, thirty years ago from when I write this. My car was loaded with clothes and typewriter (no computers then) and other things I thought I might need for the year. Once you start camping I find it gets into your blood and becomes a routine. But when you get away from it camping seems too much to handle in terms of finding a campsite, cooking, and setting up and tearing down a tent as you move along each day. Laura, Peter, and I got along together, again balancing the opposites between them and me, and between each of them who were friends, but did not have too much in common. I loved the freedom of the driving and the scenery along the way. The Rocky Mountains were beautiful. I loved and was awed by the wild flowers growing in the national parks we visited. I think if I recall we lucked out with not too much rain to contend with. As I think of what was significant about this journey besides the natural beauty, the message that comes is that we made it and made it together with no big clashes or crashes.

We arrived at St. Mary Magdalen and I got settled in. Each of them went their separate ways which were the plans we all had when we began our journey together. I took my time in getting settled in. Father Sullivan was, in comparison to what I was used to in Minnesota, pretty conservative, as was the Archdiocese of Los Angeles. To my understanding the Archdiocese, which was dominated from its beginning by a strong conservative Irish influence, had really lost touch or turned off many of the more creative, liberal, intelligent but wonderful loving people of Southern California. This local church, like all of them and each of us, was dealing with the tension of opposites. The challenge was how to hold the tension of the opposites between the more conservative traditional church of Vatican I and the coming forth of the more creative life-filled spirit of the Vatican II church.

St. Mary Magdalen friends - left to right - Dr. Mayenne Keralitz, Francesca de Franco, me, Helen Richards

St. Mary Magdalen had an ideal location bordering Beverly Hills and Hollywood Hills. It was also very close to Santa Monica Beach area and not that far from downtown Los Angeles. It took me time to catch my breath and to find my way around. I loved the easy access to Santa Monica Beach and made use of it. In those days I was more of a beach bum and sun worshiper. I was not in immediate contact with Hal at the Center. Little did I know that Hal was moving out of the Center after draining his own personal resources to make the Center happen. But I got involved and Hal included me in whatever was available with what I felt I needed. He welcomed me in his plans to move on and did not leave me stranded.

I was blessed over the years in being connected with Hal and the Center. I met so many extraordinary and dedicated people concerned about consciousness and personal and spiritual growth and grounded in the

Dr. Julian Keralitz another dear friend from St. Mary Magdalen

earth as was Hal. I was fascinated by Robert Gerard and Integral Psychology and studied under him, as well as taking many other opportunities to grow and learn. Many friends in Minnesota thought when I left for Los Angeles I would not come back. If I did come back I would not come back as a priest. Yet all these experiences enhanced my priesthood and all those I met respected me and my priesthood. They were excited that a priest was interested in all this important work of psychological spiritual growth in consciousness and holistic health and healing.

Besides all the contacts at the Center for the Healing Arts, I met some wonderful people who were members of the parish. They were good to me and, I to them. They also encouraged me to bring about more openness and creative spirit in the parish. These qualities were not so important to Father Sullivan as pastor, so here again was a challenge for me to balance the opposites in me and in the parish community. This balancing act went well.

This year went by very fast, too fast. I was blessed to have some friends and family come to visit me during this year. I loved the climate of Los Angeles and the friendly open spirit of the people. I felt sad to leave, but it was time to go home and I agree, there is no place like home. Before I go home with you, in the next chapter I will share with you what was going on within me as far as spiritual growth and consciousness development.

My Year With Hal and Sidra Stone

CHAPTER TEN

The Center For Healing Arts
1978-1979

Minds are like parachutes –
they don't work unless they are open.

I would say hearts are the same way. If they don't open they don't give out love or receive it. While in Los Angeles, I trusted, took a risk, kept my heart and mind open, and learned much. I met many wonderful, gifted, and humble people who kept their hearts and minds open as well. Before I share my next experience back in Minnesota, I share here how I have grown and how I keep growing as I continue my life journey.

Through the clinical pastoral education program at Hazelden, the summer conferences sponsored by the Center for the Healing Arts, and my year with Hal and his staff at the Center, my mind and heart expanded immensely in understanding the Psycho-Spiritual world. Looking at the total person and circumstances of his/her life is needed for healing and recovery. The same are needed for living a full life as we make our life journey on planet earth.

From the Center for the Healing Arts, Hal and his wife Sidra moved on to discovering and developing their teaching on the *Psychology of Selves* and the *Aware Ego*. The process side of this theory was Voice Dialogue. We are made up of many selves who run our lives and make our decisions. These selves can often lead us into illness or a fuller experience of life and health and recovery.

To my mind and heart, this teaching is the best I have come across to help me understand myself and others and the healing process. Through our family systems and other circumstances of our lives, we develop many selves. The ones who dominate our lives are primary and the ones we suppress are disowned. Health and recovery are the balance between these two opposites. Hal and Sidra have named this theory the Psychology of the *Aware Ego*. The *Aware Ego* comes about as we discover and experience our primary selves and also discover and experience their opposites, our disowned selves. The *Aware Ego* holds the tension of these opposites and gives us choice in our lives. If we do not experience both opposites, the primary self or selves run our lives and make our choices, which are not really choices, since we do not know the opposite which is needed for choice.

As I mentioned earlier, when I was at the Church of St. Matthew and even Maternity of Mary, I was experiencing many opposites in parish life and in the broader life of church, country, and world. My sense in looking back is that I did not know about the *Psychology of Selves/Aware Ego* and *Voice Dialogue*, but I had an *Aware Ego* process functioning in my life to survive and live the challenges of all the opposites I was exposed to. The *Aware Ego* not only holds the tension of the opposites, but also connects us back to the cave of our heart. There we meet our vulnerable child, our unique identity, our feelings and emotions, and our deeper connection with God. God's love is poured forth in our hearts by the Holy Spirit, as Paul teaches in Romans 5, and as the Hindu teaching suggests, loves us all in silence.

I need to speak more about Voice Dialogue, which Hal and Sidra developed as the process to contact and meet our primary and disowned selves. In meeting our selves, we get to experience them, to separate from them, and allow the *Aware Ego* to develop between them. This then allows freedom and choice.

A brief explanation of the process of *Voice Dialogue* is this: You sit and discuss with the client or person you are working with what selves are big in their lives. You help them to get an awareness that they and we all are made up of many selves. (Most people do not know we are made up of many selves.) Some of the more common selves are: Pleaser, Pusher, Perfectionist, Critic, Rational Mind, and others. When the client has become aware (with your help) of who is the primary self or selves running his/her life, you invite him or her to move the chair to that self. When they have moved, you talk with that self as another person inside of them. What happens when they move their chair is that the person or self appears, and you have a conversation with the self as another person which that self is. It is an amazing process and needs to be experienced to really appreciate what I am talking about here. After some time in meeting the primary self, the next step needs to be taken. When you and the client are ready, you have the client move the chair to the opposite side and meet the disowned self. The person who you are working with may not even know this self is there.

Over a period of time with this process of meeting the opposites, an *Aware Ego* develops, holding the balance of these two opposites and allowing choice and freedom. Along with this come insight and a connection to our deeper self and God in the cave of the heart. This is a brief description and I hope somewhat helpful. Many books and DVD's and other teaching helps by Hal and Sidra are available for those interested in a more in-depth learning experience.

The *Aware Ego* makes choices and guides us on our life journey, which in one sense is the process of developing our Unique *Aware Ego*. This to my mind is the light that leads us on our life journey and keeps us balanced, holding the tension of the many opposites that are a part of our lives.

After my year with Hal at the Center for the Healing Arts, my priesthood was enhanced, not lost. It was time to go back to Minnesota and the Archdiocese of St. Paul and Minneapolis. I was committed there as priest and so I returned. At this time and even now I find no contradictions between all I learned and the message of the Gospel of Jesus Christ. This Gospel message which I was and am committed to, I continue to proclaim. I also find it even more challenging as I live it out in my daily life. So come back to Minnesota with me.

CHAPTER ELEVEN

**Church of St. Edward
1979-1982**

**Know that your true home
is in the Holy Presence.**

I came back home to Minnesota to find the Holy Presence and my home in the Church of St. Edward in West Bloomington. Again this was a challenge of opposites—coming from a small rather conservative Church of St. Mary Magdalen to a large more liberal suburban church in West Bloomington, a suburb of Minneapolis. When I arrived the parish had the title of "The Flag Ship" of the Archdiocese. I came and did not do much, but lots of things happened. There was a large professional staff. With this situation came the usual challenges of a large staff and the territory ownership that comes with it. I am not a big suburban guy as I came from a small town in Minnesota. This was a challenge of balance for me personally and a balance between the different groups in the parish. All these groups expected and needed attention. They held a many-faceted view of what the church is, should be, and could be. There was a mixture of Vatican I church and Vatican II church and much in between. There was much interest in what I had learned in California. For some it was extremely too liberal and unorthodox. For others it was exciting, challenging, and growth-provoking. Again back to the need for balance and an *Aware Ego* to discern and make good choices. There is in all of us a conservative Christian and also a liberal Christian, but many do not own both with balance. Usually we own just one of these opposites and disown the other. When only one opposite is owned, this results in polarization, conflict, disagreement, hurt feelings and sometimes the decision to leave the parish. One big primary self in all of us, and especially in a pastor, is a Pleaser. I have a big one. I also can say no and mean it. A pastor without the access to "Mr. No," as I call him, is in big trouble. In no way can you please everybody in a large varied Christian community. I like the Twelve Step slogan which says the same thing: "Formula for failure: trying to please everyone." This applied here and maybe more so because the parish was young and large, with lots of energy to energize both opposites.

Because of the large size of St. Edward's a new neighboring parish, Pax Christi, was started in Eden Prairie. Tim Power, who was a very popular previous pastor, was appointed as pastor of Pax Christi. As a result a large number of people knowing Tim from St. Edward's joined the new parish. This created some conflict and tension. Along with this was some loss of good leadership and income.

As I mentioned, the parish had a large and very professional staff.

Not all the staff agreed with each other or with me or with some of the leadership in the community. So some of the staff left, some were asked to leave, and I was caught in the middle attempting to hold the tension of the opposites. Actually I did pretty well. When all the storms were somewhat over and dust settled, I was still there as pastor. At this point it was my discernment to move on as pastor, because I carried some of the remnants and scars of the "battle" between opposites, if you want to call it that. By moving on I would be free, and the parish with the new pastor would be free to begin again.

In one sense, I made a foolish mistake as sometimes happens in my life. I resigned as pastor with no "new job" to go to. This is not too bright, at least in the business world, and even the church. Where do I go next? God is good and took care of me again, and maybe again my high faith and trust level came to my rescue.

The Church of St. Bridget of Sweden in the small community of Lindstrom was in need of a new pastor and it appealed to me because it was smaller. The big attraction also was access to Hazelden, one of the best treatment and training centers in the world. Some gave it the title the "Cadillac of treatment centers," not because of money but because of quality of care. Hazelden was within the parish boundaries. This would provide for me an opportunity to explore again my interest in helping people find healing and recovery. To get the assignment I had to work on Archbishop Roach. I also got some help from Hazelden contacts like Gordy Grimm. They knew me and they wanted a pastor at St. Bridget's open to the ministry of Hazelden and the recovery journey of persons living with addictions. My getting the appointment had another hurtle to overcome. The Priest Personnel Board at the time wanted to put someone else in there. But probably due to Archbishop Roach and God, I received the assignment. The pastor who was leaving St. Bridget's preceded me once before, at St. Pius X in White Bear Lake. Again I would say we were a contrast in opposites. The energy he held in the parish and the energy I would bring in was pretty opposite. Thanks to my *Aware Ego*, I managed to keep some balance. There was another challenge of opposites, which I was not quite ready for. I came from St. Edward's, which had a large and very competent staff, but at St. Bridget's I could not find a secretary to put out a parish bulletin in the very poorly equipped office. The church was small, and liturgy seemed not very uplifting after coming from the high quality offered at St. Edward's. The parish was in the midst of many lakes, so there was a summer crowd of parishioners and then the regular year-round members. My stay at St. Edward's was the shortest of any parish stay, with the exception of St. Mary Magdalen in West L. A.

I was writing the original draft of this chapter when I was traveling out

Kay and Jack Jasper who helped me weather the storms at St. Edwards and are still dear friends today

of the country on one of my Fr. Gulliver journeys to the Third World. When I got home to New Hope, I rediscovered a gift I received from St. Edward's on my leaving the parish. The gift was a bound copy of all my Parish Bulletin columns as Pastor. I wrote these as a regular weekly communication channel with the large parish community. As I looked over, them I was amazed at all the different topics that I wrote about and how well I wrote. But also in the back of this book of bulletins was a two-page statement of the Accountability of my Stewardship written on June 13, l982. In rereading this Accountability Statement I was amazed at all we had accomplished together in my short three years at St. Ed's.

I have no intention of sharing this lengthy statement with you, but will share the final paragraph of the statement.

"During my pastoral leadership, the Parish of St. Edward's has grown. I have listed for you some of the areas of growth. Many areas of spiritual growth are not very tangible and measurable. I am sure growth has happened far beyond our ability to see, to touch and feel it. I share with you the words of one parishioner which touches on this. 'We feel that your stay had a measure of difficulty that you overcame. It also provided growth for those who chose to accept the challenge. We heard many messages in your sermons which served us well, and for that we are grateful.'

Many Thanks to all of you – through your ownership and accountability you have made St. Edward's the great parish that it is, and will continue to be. Fr. Bill Whittier"

When I left I shared again the message of Cardinal Newman from his sermon, "The Parting of Friends." This time it remained in the bulletin since I was the Pastor and did not delete it, as was the case in my first parish of Maternity of Mary.

CHAPTER TWELVE

**Church of St. Bridget Of Sweden
and Hazelden
1982-1994**

One day at a time.

St. Bridget of Sweden called for lots of renewal, so it was important to take one day at a time. My Pusher saw much to do and wanted it done yesterday. At the beginning of my new pastoral ministry, I had not the energy, and the community had not been called to life to help facilitate the necessary renewal. The rectory was adequate and with some work would house me and also some trainees from the Hazelden training programs. At one time we had two trainees living in the lower basement level and one in the guest room upstairs. In the more remote past the house had been built to serve this purpose as there was in the earlier day's good cooperation between Hazelden and St. Bridget's. Soon after I arrived, I was looking for the washing machine but could not find it anywhere in the house. But looking more closely, I saw that there was a small room between two other rooms in the basement. I opened the door and there was the washing machine. Part of the challenge for me was to find my way around the house which had many rooms and a basement full of little hidden rooms. This kept me out of trouble and gave my pusher something to do.

The Church space was inadequate. There was very small office space. Another inadequacy was there were no classroom space for the Religious Education of our young people. The previous pastor said that Religious Education of their children was the parents' responsibility, so no classes were offered. Many parents saw the need for more religious education provided by the parish community, as I did. Since we had no educational spaces we rented the public school for classes. This worked as a temporary solution. The previous pastor did not put priority on religious education, but he saved some money. As we started to come alive as a community, we had some money to work with. We were able to think seriously about some additional building for education and also a more suitable worship space. As the community came alive and were invited and in-

Vicki McNally and me

70

volved in the life of the parish, we got organized—a Parish Council, a Finance Committee, a Religious Education Committee, a Liturgy Committee, and also a Building Committee to look at a more suitable worship space and some educational and office space—all became part of the life of the parish community.

Some basic staff was needed to handle the office work and also be involved in Religious Education Formation. I sat down with a friend who helped me in many ways at St. Pius X, Jeanne Farrell. Our task was to interview possible secretaries. She recommended one, and I recommended Vicki McNally. Vicki got the job. Later on my friend Jeanne agreed that I made the correct choice. Vicki is still involved as Parish Administrator to this day, 27 years later. She grew and the parish grew and

Eileen and John Silver

we all grew together. I invited Lois Rather, also from St. Pius X, to help Vicki and me to get the financial books in order. She was the bookkeeper, and a good one, when I was Pastor at St. Pius X in White Bear Lake. Lois was a diabetic from an early age, and I always marveled how she took such good care of herself. As well as taking care of herself, she knew how to take good care of the financial books. She was a big help to us at St. Bridget's. She also did my business cards for me, as well as offered to edit this autobiography. She had to stop editing after doing the first chapter because her diabetes was acting up. Lois ended up in the hospital and died in her sleep from a heart attack. I was in Uganda at the time so I could not be at her funeral.

Eileen Silver took the lead with Religious Education, along with others who wanted the best education possible for our young people. I think often with sadness and tears of Eileen Silver and her husband John, who both died young. They were such a big part of getting things moving for Religious Education. They spent much time with me before I decided to

Frank and Janet Hofmann supervised with care and diligence all our building projects. Janet helped supervise household needs.

come to St. Bridget's, encouraging me to come as pastor. At this time there were no what you would call professional staff. We had parishioners who came forward to organize, call to life and grow themselves as staff. Life happened, and as the Community came alive, new buildings came alive to meet our needs. An Educational facility, an office facility, and a beautiful new church attached to the old church were all built. The old church became a needed social hall. These beautiful and needed additions changed the landscape of the property the parish owned along Highway eight across from the Lindstrom landmark, the Dairy Queen.

As this life was happening the parish rectory got some needed remodeling. Trainees from Hazelden were invited to share my home and, if they were priests, to help preside at worship on weekends. The first to come was Father Jacob Yali, who was studying at Hazelden and needed a home away from his home in Jos, Nigeria, in West Africa. Jacob, who was a very black Nigerian, added some color to our community and was well liked. If people had an issue with his skin color or other Nigerian habits in our all-white community and parish, Jacob had a laugh that won over the hardest and most biased of hearts. After Jacob, others came to share my home. This provided a wonderful expanded family for both me and our Parish Community. Also when the Renewal Center was finished at Hazelden, I was invited to offer a class on journaling for those coming for Renewal. Hazelden also provided transportation for any clients from Hazelden who wanted to worship on Sunday and in my time even daily Mass. I enjoyed watching the clients from Hazelden every Sunday be transformed as their treatment progressed for the four weeks. Each Sunday they came looking more alive and happy and full of joy and gratitude. Many of them had not been inside a Catholic Church for years and were concerned the roof might fall in on them. Happy to say the roof did not fall in but sheltered them well.

The Catholic Church is International, but my International connection came more through Hazelden, which drew clients and trainees from all

Roland, me and Leo, friends from extended care at Hazelden. Carol is seated in front of her husband Roland, Anita, Leo's wife seated in front of me and Leo.

over the world. I met wonderful clients and made special friends with some who were in extended care, where they stayed longer than the 28 days.

There were three persons who were in extended care at Hazelden who became special friends of mine, and still are even to this day. Louise, one of the three, died from relapse going back home to an environment that was not conducive to health and recovery. Families share in the disease of addiction and when they do not do their homework on getting healthy, they can often be the cause of relapse for recovering persons going back home. Louise was a gentle, generous, beautiful lady and dear friend, and her death broke my heart. This is the downside of getting too close to persons in recovery, for all life is fragile but theirs is more so. Leo and Roland, the other two of the three who are alive and well, are still very dear friends

Mary and John Lelwica

who I have regular contact with. I have found you cannot have a better friend than one who is in recovery. They are honest, open, generous and always there for you if you need them.

Two other dear people and friends I need to mention are John and Mary Lelwica. They came to the parish about the time I did, and were generous in getting involved in the parish in many different ways. They had a special connection to me since Mary was an excellent cook and I was invited often or invited myself to their home for dinner. This was especially helpful for me, since I had no cook and needed a meal after the 5 PM Mass on Saturday night. Also they were most generous in allowing me to invite trainees from Hazelden and others as dinner guests to join us. You could not find a meal in the best restaurant in the world to match the meal Mary prepared. I remember one incident which was a little embarrassing at first. I invited a young Indian woman trainee from Hazelden to join us. I goofed in not realizing that she was a vegetarian until we sat down at table. But this was dealt with easily, since along with an excellent meat entre Mary always had plenty of delicious vegetables and salad which would suffice for a vegetarian dinner. The salad was more than sufficient. Mary does not cook much now so we meet for dinner, when I am home, at The Dock in Stillwater which serves excellent food. But I still feel Mary out did them with her cooking. Also my bringing guests to their table opened their lives in many ways and provided exciting conversation as well as providing new friends for them. It was John who gave me the

Father Bill in front of Our Lady of Victory rehabilitation center in Jos, Nigera

title of Fr. Gulliver as I set off on my international traveling. I have always loved the metaphor and it fits me well in many ways.

The trainees at Hazelden were international. Some lived with me and others I met through those who lived with me. Father Jacob went back to Jos, Nigeria,

and established, Our Lady of Victory, the first treatment center in West Africa following the Hazelden model of recovery based on the 12 Steps of AA. Jacob invited me to come to Nigeria and help him with establishing the rehab. I took my educational and holiday time and went off to Nigeria to help Jacob. When clients in the rehab in Nigeria were open to it, I would offer some of the teaching of the Psychology of *Aware Ego* and *Voice dialogue* process to help them. This process helped them to get more clarity on their recovery process. Father Joe Pereira, the founder and managing trustee of Kripa, a large rehab organization for alcoholics and addicts in India, came for some training at Hazelden. Father Joe, having heard I had gone to Nigeria, invited me to come to India as well. Sister Margaret studied at Hazelden and established Tabor Lodge in Cork, Ireland. Some of her staff lived with me, so here was the Ireland connection. Along with this our parish community continued to come alive and grow. A new beautiful church appeared on Highway 8 and behind it sprung up educational classrooms and office facilities.

Along with this I kept my connection with Hal and Sidra Stone and was on some of their staffs for Summer Camp. I kept growing in their work. There was always something new Hal and Sidra were discovering in their work. This added new life and light to their teaching and to my life. As

the saying goes, "no dust collected on them" or on those who followed them and their ongoing teaching.

In 1992 I took up Father Joe's invitation to visit Kripa in India. My international life was expanding. As I did for Nigeria, I used my educational and holiday time to visit India.

Mother Teresa sits on the floor in their chapel and shares her love and wisdom with us. Fr. Joe sits to her left and I took the picture.

With priest trainees living with me, I had enough help at the parish to cover my ministry when I went to Nigeria and India. During my first visit with Kripa in India, the staff had gathered in Calcutta (now known as Kolkata) for a training session. This session was for all the staff from the many different rehab centers run by Kripa. Father Joe was with us, and we had on this visit the special privilege to visit Mother Teresa's Mother House. Fr. Joe and Mother Teresa were close friends and shared some common ministry together. She is the inspiration for Kripa's ministry. An added blessing was that Mother Teresa was home and we were able to meet with her. We all sat on the floor of the chapel. Mother Teresa sat on the floor in the middle of all of us sharing her love and wisdom with us. This was a special treat for all the staff of Kripa and especially for me on my first visit to India.

My length of tenure as pastor at St. Bridget's was running out. I was expected to stay 12 years, and they were coming to a close. What do I do now? This was the longest I had ever stayed in one parish as pastor or associate pastor and now it was time to move on. I had many international connections with Hazelden, Hal and Sidra Stone, the Catholic Church, my personal visits to Nigeria and India, plus my childhood interest in geography. The message came to me that my next step in my life journey was to take on an international challenge to help the third world.

How would this be possible with my commitment to be a priest in the Archdiocese of St. Paul and Minneapolis?

The best way to explore this call would be to discuss the matter with Archbishop Roach. Father Bill Baumgaertner, from my college Logic class and Seminary days, was consulted. He gave me some suggestions and encouragement how best to approach the Archbishop on this matter close to my heart.

I went to see Archbishop Roach and shared my call with him. With some reluctance he gave me permission to go to India, and also assured me I would always be welcome to come back and serve in the Archdiocese. My sense was Archbishop Roach felt that what our Archdiocese shared would come back in many ways to bless us, and it did.

Fr. Jacob Yali and Fr. Bill

So in July 1994 I left St. Bridget's to go off to India with the intention of staying on there, serving with Kripa. So one step in my life journey ended, and I began a new step in my life journey to find myself, my own wisdom, and my God. I felt very sad to leave St. Bridget's, my beloved home for 12 years. However I knew in my heart I was making the correct decision. I discovered to my surprise there was some anger from some of the parishioners at St. Bridget's in that they expected me to stay on as their pastor until my retirement or maybe retire there as a reasonable choice or goal. Needless to say a pastor never pleases everyone, so along with anger and sadness, some were delighted I was moving on. Again many selves in me were involved and my *Aware Ego* had to balance the emotions and opposites involved. When the choice was made, it felt to me to be the cor-

25th Anniversary of Ordination celebration

rect choice. My high school interest in international geography was coming to life in me. Also Indian mentors like Gandhi, and Bede Griffiths, and even Mother Teresa along with my commitment to the Gospel of Jesus were moving me along this step of my life journey to serve the poor in India.

Before I close this chapter of my life journey at St. Bridget of Sweden, I need to include two very special events during this time. One event is the celebration of 25 years of ordination as a Catholic priest on June 8, 1986. The other event is the death of my mother on January 10, 1988.

Let us first explore briefly the 25th celebration of my ordination as a Catholic priest. The liturgy was longer than I expected for two reasons. 1. We had lots of good music, and I enjoy good music in the Liturgy. 2. I wanted to have a shared homily, having someone from each step of my journey in life to share a reflection. This began with Farmington and included the Seminary and all the parishes I had ministered at for these 25 years. This took much longer than I expected, so the Liturgy was long and held up the reception after. Bill Yaeger and his beloved wife Dar, who was struggling with brain cancer, insisted they have a party for me at their lake home separate from the reception. The guests would be my family, close friends, out-of-town guests, and some of the people from St. Bridget's who were very close to me or involved in ministry with me. This was a lovely celebration, overlooking North Lindstrom Lake with the weather smiling on us. The pig roast was excellent and we let balloons go into a lovely blue sky to signify the beauty, freedom, and spiritual aspect of the celebration. I am forever grateful to Bill and Dar for this lovely gesture of hospitality for my immediate family and out-of-town friends, some coming from as far away as California. Since then Dar has gone home to God. Her leaving us was not too long after the celebration. Dar was in need of much help, besides the dedicated care given her by her devoted husband

Thank You

I extend my heartfelt thanks to:

Bill and Dar Yaeger for the pig roast and party for my out-of-town guests and relatives on Saturday.

Bill. She had many people from the parish as well as me to help care for her. She called us her shepherds. She gave each of us a beautiful little statue of the boy shepherd with the sheep on his shoulder. To this day I treasure this gift, and it travels with me wherever I go as part of my traveling meditation altar. It stands before me now as I type this chapter. Bill also had a good shepherd statue placed in front of the entrance of the church in memory of Dar.

The second event I want and need to share is the death of my mother.

On January 10, 1988, I received a call from the caretaker in the apartment in Farmington where my mother lived. He told me the sad news that he found my mother dead in her apartment. When the communion minister came to give my mother communion, she did not get the usual response when she called my mother. She informed the caretaker, and opening the apartment, he found my mother had died. I told the caretaker when he called to leave everything as it was until I came there from Lindstrom, which was about an hour's drive. I arrived to see a very touching and beautiful scene for me personally. My mother lay curled up on the floor of her bedroom like a little child, with her head on her favorite traveling pillow and her rosary in hand. Whenever my mother would travel in later years, mostly to come and stay a few days with me, she always would bring her own pillow and rosary. Here she was now with her traveling pillow and rosary journeying home to be with God, her husband, and other family and friends who had gone before her. We had talked often about death. I along with her was ready to meet her death when God called. Our family was ready as well. I particularly, and the rest of my family, spent much time with her so she was never neglected by family or friends. Although I am not sure what happened that night, I told her before that if she was ready to go, do not call 911 because if you do they will not let you die. She did not call them, and she died. I would say she died the way she wanted to. This was a special gift to me and our family. I need to admit though I miss her very much. I see more clearly the importance of the mother in a family. She is with me in spirit when I write this autobiography. Many a time as I have questions about family and growing up I wish she was here to consult and ask her suggestions and seek her wisdom. Also I appreciate even more all she did for our family and the pain and suffering she underwent out of love for us and the God she loved and served. She died with the Rosary in her hands and Mary was a significant source of strength for her. I could not close this chapter of my life without sharing those two added events during my sojourn at the Church of St. Bridget in Lindstrom, Minnesota.

Good Shepherd statue outside of St. Bridget of Sweden's front door of the church, donated by Bill Yaeger in memory of Dar.

Me standing in front of the Taj Mahal in Agra

CHAPTER THIRTEEN

Off to India - KRIPA
1994-1996

Let go and let God

I n my high school geography class we/I made a plaster relief map of the world with the Himalaya Mountains towering above India. Years later, I made two visits to India. Now I was going for what seemed at the time a committed stay for life. Maybe I would finally see the Himalaya Mountains that I formed out of plaster back in my high school days?

This decision to go to India was really letting go and letting God. Many thought I was a little crazy and maybe I was. With trust in God I packed up and disposed of my belongings at St. Bridget's. With both sadness and joy (and relief as well), I said goodbye and thank you to St. Bridget of Sweden Church. These were twelve challenging, sometimes very painful but exciting and fulfilling years of ministry. St. Bridget of Sweden was and still is a lovely parish community and a home to me.

As I mentioned earlier Hal and Sidra Stone made me aware that we are made up of many selves. John Lelwica named the self I was into as I went off to India. The name he gave the self was "Fr. Gulliver." I was off like Gulliver traveling to meet and serve the little people of the world.

Back 45 years ago when I was at the Church of St. Matthew, the students in the school named another self for me, "Sunshine." Since then Gloria Carpenter has helped me keep that self alive and shining. Her daughter Kim named another self the "Hippie Priest." As I traveled, new selves were discovered and named by me or by others I met on my journey.

As part of keeping in contact with family and friends, I would send out a newsletter periodically and sign it Fr. Gulliver, alias Fr. Bill and name some of the other selves.

Father Gulliver is now off to India. I left the Twin Cities in the afternoon on an NWA overnight flight. It arrived in Amsterdam in the early morning. Later that morning I caught a KLM flight to Mumbai. There I was met around 1:00 a.m. by some of the Kripa staff. I would be freezing with extra clothes on in the long international flights. Many passengers around me would be in shorts and tee shirt. Here I would be wearing a turtle neck shirt with a tee shirt underneath. On top of these I would wear a vest. All of these to keep me warm. Besides all this I often would ask for extra blankets as well. Friends of mine tell me to put on more weight and I will not freeze so much. I prefer less weight and the extra blankets. Upon leaving the airport in hot humid Mumbai I needed to strip down to a tee shirt to keep cool. In my early days I traveled very light with one carry on suitcase. Going to a warm country and not needing a lot of dress up clothes made it easier to travel light. I also remember many years ago at a retreat in Canada this little tidbit of wisdom. "To follow the Light travel light." I honored this best I could and it worked at least for me. So my regular flights back and forth to Mumbai would follow the schedule I just described. KLM was my favorite airline for food, comfort and service. In later years NWA took over the KLM flight to Mumbai, which was a disappointment to me.

Fr. Bill with Fr. Joe Pereira at Kripa in Vasai.

In one of my previous visits to India, Father Joe made sure I flew to Delhi and then on to Agra to see the famous Taj Mahal. A Jesuit priest friend of Father Joe's met me and was my guide. Moving amongst bicycle rickshaws and much traffic we found the Taj. I was amazed at its unique beauty. I can see why it is considered one of the Seven Wonders of the World. We then went from the Taj to stay with the Jesuit priests at their residence. I will never forget how Agra was extremely hot in the day time but extremely cold and full of mosquitoes at night. Because of its elevation you had these changes in temperature. This was a combination I was not used to from Minnesota. In my home in Minnesota we have mosquitoes, but in the hot summer time. An added luxury we have in Minnesota is we have plenty of screens on our windows. The screens keep the rascals outside. That night in Agra was a challenge to get some sleep. I got very little in fact. The Jesuits had many schools in Agra and elsewhere in India. I was surprised that most of their students were not Catholic. Unlike the USA where all our Catholic schools are pretty well filled with Catholic students, the majority of the students here in India are Hindu or Muslim. This would reflect the population ratio. The Catholic Church has and is providing a wonderful educational service to

India. Unfortunately this service is not always appreciated. The Hindus and Muslims were not converted but learned much about Christianity. Often times they were more knowledgeable than the Catholics about the Catholic Faith.

But back to my decision to stay in India after I left St. Bridget of Sweden. In one of my earlier visits as I mentioned I had already met Mother Teresa. When people hear me say that I have met Mother Teresa, I am often asked what Mother was like. I describe her in this way with all due respect and honor. She reminded me of a loving, humble, and wise grandmother who was gifted with the ability to be present in the moment. This meant when you met her she was right there with you. You felt her loving presence. Being present in the moment meant she was present to God, to life, to grace, to you and of course to herself. Another way to express this is to say she possessed the unique gift of Mindfulness. What a gift when she had a million other things to be present to. Right at this moment she was present to you.

Fr Bill calling on Mother Teresa at home, note doorbell and name plate.

If you could take a peek inside Mother Teresa's heart I suspect you would find written in gentle and bold letters the words of Jesus in the Judgment Scene of the Gospel described in Matthew 25.

A paraphrase of the text is, "I was hungry and you gave me to eat and thirsty you gave me to drink....What you do to the least of my brothers or sisters you do unto me."

To my mind and heart this is how Mother Teresa saw the world and everyone in it. She responded accordingly with eyes of faith. She saw Jesus in everyone she met but especially in the poor and needy. She seemed to

Fr. Bill gifting Hal and Sidra's book, "Embracing Ourselves" to Mother Teresa.

know and live out Paul's teaching on the Risen Cosmic Christ. The Risen Cosmic Christ is in all of creation and especially in the little people, the poor. As Tony de Mello, S.J. would put it in his book *Call to Love*, "To see is to Love." Mother could see. Another reminder of Mother Teresa is from many years ago before I had met her. Senator Hatch visited her in Calcutta back maybe ten years ago or more. I heard him give a talk in Minneapolis. He shared in his talk that he asked her if she didn't get overwhelmed and discouraged with all the poor calling for help in Calcutta and the other parts of our home planet earth. Her response was simple and wise, "Be Faithful not Successful." My reflection from this is when we are faithful we are always successful. From Mother quoting some prayers of John Henry Newman, I sensed she had a special devotion to him. I had not explored how John Henry Newman fit into her life. Maybe like for me he was one of her mentors?

I did not keep much of a Journal which would have helped me write this book. One event that I did mark in my date book and kept transfer-

Green Park entry of the Missionary Sisters of Charity

ring from year to year is September 8, 1994. This was the day I offered a retreat for some of Mother's Sisters at Green Park. Green Park is one of their retreat centers near the airport in Calcutta. It is a little noisy as you might expect. I had never given a formal retreat to Religious Women before. Now here I was in India, a different country and culture, called upon to provide a Retreat for these very beautiful Missionary Sisters of Charity. Mother required in the Constitution that all the Sisters know English, so this was a big help for me to begin with. I obtained a copy of their Constitution so I could offer reflections from it, plus other reflections that seemed appropriate for the retreat. There was a saying going around that Mother would sit in on the Retreats to make sure the Retreat Master was teaching orthodox spirituality. She visited Green Park a couple of times while I was there but did not sit in on my reflections. This made me feel I met her standards for a Retreat Master. The Sisters in retreat responded beautifully. I was kept very busy keeping up with what was best to offer for the daily reflections and meditations. Besides the Retreat facility Green Park provided two other ministries to the people. 1. They provided food supplies for the needy. 2. They took care of the sick babies in a beautiful nursery. I loved to visit the nursery and enjoy the babies. When the babies were well enough they were returned to their parents. With all the

A line for food inside the compound

poverty and hot weather I always marveled how well all of Mother's facilities were kept clean and as cool as could be provided, mostly with fans.

I always remember with some embarrassment when I offered Mass for the Sisters. I would have a fan over the altar for me. They lived a simpler life with no fan over them. If you were their guest for a meal you were fed well and they ate a very simple fare. The Sisters were very good about practicing what they preach or as we say now, walking the talk.

I was curious about what brought Father Joe and Mother Teresa together. I was told the story that Father Joe and the Kripa facility had called back to life some men left at Mother's doorstep drunk or close to death. One of Kripa's present staff is one of these men. Mother and her Community are to this day an inspiration to Father Joe and Kripa and to me as well.

While in Mumbai with Kripa I met and made some new friends. Aaron Pereira was Ossie's son. Pereira is a very common Portuguese name in this area. This is the same name of Fr. Joe's family name. They are not related. Ossie at the time was the Center Manager of Kripa Mumbai. Ossie was a recovering alcoholic who Fr. Joe in the early days brought back to life. As alcoholism is a family disease, Aaron was one of the three sons

Fr. Joy came to learn about Kripa

most affected by the disease. We became close friends. Aaron opened up and blossomed into a fuller and joy-filled life. He is now married and has a good job. He and his lovely wife Tina are praying for a baby to arrive. We are still dear friends and correspond by email. Another friend I met was Fr. Joy a priest from south India. Fr. Joy came to Mumbai to study the program at Kripa. We in turn became dear friends and he called to life another self in me called "Papa." Fr. Joy is presently living and ministering in New York with plans to return to his home in South India. Another friend who I keep in almost daily email contact with even today is Dr. Rani Raote. She studied in the USA and got her PhD in Psychology. She then chose to return to India. Many in her position would definitely have chosen to stay in the USA. Women have much more respect and better opportunities in the USA than in India. But no, Dr.Rani brought her counseling skills back home to help those in need in India. There are few well trained psychotherapists in India so her skills were very much needed. She came to work part time in Kripa at about the same time I arrived there. This is how we met. Her education in the USA and her professional skills in counseling provided us with a common ground of interest. She has since left Kripa and moved on to her own private practice and teaching. Besides this she has a lovely husband, Sanjay. I always admire how she is always open to learn and grow. She takes all the opportunities that are available to do so in India and online. Besides being a close friend she is to this day an inspiration to me to keep growing and learning.

Part of my role in Kripa would be to visit some of their rehab centers which were mostly located in the northern half of India. I would spend time with staff and clients helping in any way I could. With my expertise in Hal and Sidra's teaching of the *Aware Ego* and the *Voice Dialogue* process I would share this with the Centers. I would share with both clients and staff. This was more of a challenge since I only knew English and many of the clients and some staff did not know English. So there was a need for a translator when I would give the input teaching sessions. The plus side of this is those who knew English got the message twice and this helped them understand better. Another challenge to me and to them was that some of my teaching was a little foreign to their language and culture. But we moved ahead and learned from each other.

One of the Centers was in Darjeeling which is the "Queen of the Hills" and at the foothills of

Dr. Rani Raote

the Himalayas. As I visited the different Kripa centers it was time to go to Darjeeling. To get to Darjeeling you had to fly into Bagdogra and then take a jeep or van up the steep and scary climb to Darjeeling. If you have anxiety attacks or cannot tolerate high and scary heights you best stay down in the plains at Bagdogra. The road is steep and narrow and you meet jeeps and vans packed—and I mean packed—with people coming and going. Some of the young guys would hang on the back or even be on the roof. There are all along sheer drop-offs next to the narrow road. If you are coming down you give the right away to the vehicle coming up. As you approach Darjeeling there is a large welcome sign, "The Queen of the Hills." Past the sign as you turn the corner you see a majestic and awesome sight, a Buddhist Monastery. The monastery faces you on the right side of the hill. The son of one of the staff of Kripa Darjeeling is a young monk in the monastery. During one of my initial visits to Darjeeling I took the opportunity to visit the monastery with the young monk's grandfather. It was a beautiful sacred place both on the inside and the outside. As

Welcome to Kripa Center in Vasai, Fr. Joe's home town.

things change the young monk's father has left the Kripa staff and his grandfather has since died. After passing the Monastery you begin to approach the city. Here comes the downside as there seems to be for most everything and every place. The traffic was bumper to bumper and the pollution was high density. All the jeeps and other vehicles were pouring out black smelly exhaust smoke from their tail pipes. With much patience and surviving the high pollution level, I arrived at my Himalaya destination. I was awed by the wonder, the beauty and majesty of the Himalaya Mountains. They far surpassed in size and beauty the plaster model we made in high school. I stayed at the Bishop's House when I visited Darjeeling and Kripa. This was a large stone building something like a European castle. The rooms were very large and adequate but as you might suspect cold. There was not always hot water available and often times no water was available. Each morning I would go for my morning walk before Mass at about six a.m. There was a circular walk way around the mall and it bordered the mountains above and valleys below. One special mountain you walked by each day was Mt. Kanchenjunga, the highest mountain in India and the third highest mountain in the world. I would

Fr. Bill's 60th birthday gift from the staff at Kripa

look forward to it being visible, which was not always the case. It was always a favorite place for me to stop and pray with wonder and awe and gratitude to God for life and beauty. The mountain reflected in my mind and heart the strength, the majesty, the beauty and the awesome presence of the God of this magnificent universe of ours. God like the mountain is always present even when God seems absent. On some mornings because of cloud cover Mount Kanchenjunga seemed absent. But she was always there. Along this walkway many locals would be walking or the young ones running. The older Hindus would be walking quietly with their prayer beads in hand. There were stops along the way with gym bars which became the gym for the young men and women seeking to keep in shape.

As I mentioned before, when I visited Darjeeling I would stay at the Bishop's House. This house was also connected to the seminary. I enjoyed presiding at Mass with the young tribal seminarians so full of life. They would sing from their young hearts full of joy. Those were special days and celebrations for me. These celebrations with the seminarians

After Mass with the Seminarians at Darjeeling

were more in my early visits to Darjeeling. Being at the foothills of the Himalayas besides their magnificent beauty there was the downside. You guessed it. It is the cold, damp weather. At night I just could not get warm enough. This was a reminder of my long international flights over. I kept piling on more and more heavy blankets. They were very heavy quilts not like our lighter and warmer blankets. No electric blankets were provided. I even wore a cap in bed so my body heat would not escape through my balding head. Unlike America there was no central heating. I had access to a small electric heater, but it was in no way like a hot air or hot water furnace in Minnesota. But as we know life is not perfect anywhere on the planet. As we move around the planet we choose what pluses and what minuses we want to live with. The Kripa center was just across the mall and around 9 a.m. I would walk there for my morning sessions. There was no Bishop at the time in Darjeeling and Fr. Thomas D'Souza was the administrator. Rome wanted a local tribal bishop and so Father Stephen Lepcha was chosen. He was not excited by the appointment but agreed. Bishops do not have an easy task in our world today and in the Third World their task is even more challenging. Another date I have always

Bishop Stephen and Fr. Bill

marked in my date book is Dec. 8, 1997. This was the date of Father Stephen's consecration as Bishop. Father Stephen then and now has a special place in my heart. I even made a special trip back to Darjeeling in cold December to help him celebrate his Consecration as Bishop of Darjeeling. Besides being cold, there was the positive side. I enjoyed all the local customs surrounding his celebration. I am delighted to this day that I went, and I surprised him by my coming. With his appointment the Bagdogra diocese was formed and Father Thomas D'Souza was appointed to this Diocese in the plains.

There was another Kripa Center at Goa, "the Hawaii" of India. This is quite a contrast going from the damp and cold Himalayas to warm and often hot Goa. Goa, having lovely beaches and reasonable prices, attracted many Europeans for holiday. Goa also attracted young people looking for drugs. The young people were driving around on rented motor cycles, and the drugs were there in large numbers. I had to be careful not to get run over. Anjuna Beach was where much of the drug culture was happening. Kripa had their rehab center just a block from the beach. I love the beach and the ocean, and this provided easy access to the

Goa Kripa Center staff and clients with Fr. Bill

beach. However Kripa's role was not treating those visitors who came to enjoy drugs. Kripa treated the local alcoholics and addicts. As I walked on the beach I would get offered drugs as well. If you just let them know you are not interested they moved on and you continued your walk. Since I enjoyed the beach and also the warmer weather Kripa in Goa was a favorite place for me to be. There were two downsides here for me. The language in Goa was more of a challenge for me who only knew English. The other downside was I stayed right at the rehab which was convenient but sometimes too close for privacy.

Two health negatives came from Goa. As I mentioned I would do my early morning walk at the beach. Coming back one morning at the edge of the beach I turned my back on a dog that had been abused. He attacked me and made a nice big bite in my left ankle. There was blood flowing down my ankle and on to my sandal and foot. There was no one at the beach to see what happened. This was the downside of going out so early. No one really owned the dog so there was no owner to help me. The beach was full of dogs but they were all usually friendly and did not bother you. Lucky for me Kripa always has medical help with each cen-

Joey Carvalho, wife Olive and Baby Neil who is no baby now and very bright.

ter. I hurried back with blood dripping down my sandal on to my foot. There was no pain thank God. I immediately went to Kripa's medical facility for help and got it. There was concern about a rabies infection so I took medication for prevention. The moral of the story is, never turn your back on an abused dog. As you might suspect since this incident I am a little paranoid around dogs which was not the case before. 2. The other health negative is I got bit again but this time by a bug of some sort. This was on another visit and it bit me on my knee. As a result I got an infection that would not say goodbye to my body. I was moving on from Goa at the time so I had many different doctors along the way. They were all very helpful including the Sisters at the Catholic Medical Center in Imphal. It was not until my homeward visit to Tabor Lodge in Cork, Ireland, that the infection finally said goodbye to my body. I gladly said goodbye to it as well. But I need to say thank you God that with all my visits and travels these two incidents have been my only serious health issues.

What happened here in India and also when I went with Father Jacob to Nigeria was I met many lovely people. Some of these people were connected with the rehabs and some I met through church and other contacts. Another friend and recovering addict from Goa is Joey. We first met when he was a trainee for Kripa staff back in Mumbai. When we did initial teaching with the *Voice Dialogue* he would absolutely not buy it. He did finally see its value in helping himself and others to become aware that we are made up of selves. He also saw how some of these selves can enhance or work against our recovery. Joey now is married to Olive and has a young son Neil, who is smarter than his father. Neil will keep Joey on his toes. Joey also keeps in touch with me. Sometimes my phone will ring in the morning here in New Hope, Minnesota. To my surprise and joy it is Joey or little Neil from Goa on the other end. I keep telling them it is their turn to come visit me but have only promises so far.

I still remember when I first arrived, these recovering trainees wanted me to experience the crowded trains. Believe me the local trains are very crowded. You are packed in like sardines. The passengers are standing and sitting wherever they can find a space to be. Some are hanging out the doors. To get out you have to push your way through the standing crowd and guard your wallet or other luggage. My training as weak side tackle on our high school football team came in handy. The young guys with their high and youthful energy would help me push and shove. We had to move fast so we would make it out before the train moved on to the next station. Now that I have grown "younger," I will pass on needing anymore of that experience. These experiences and many others as I have mentioned have resulted in my having many friends in these countries. Many had become like family to me then. Even today some of us are still connected which is a gift to me and to them.

These words of wisdom from the 12 Step programs come to me now. "Decisions aren't forever." My initial decision to stay on in India was changing. Father Joe and I, as happens when two people work together, did not always see eye to eye. The issue concerned my freedom to see who I wanted to see and those who wanted to see me. With this difference between us I made the decision to go back to Minnesota and I did. Aaron who worked for a moving company helped me pack to leave with sadness in both of our hearts.

Before I end this chapter on India I need to mention that through Fr. Joe I met another mentor. Fr. Joe recommended a book by Tony de Mello, S.J. entitled, *Call to Love*. With this book Tony entered my family of mentors. I was hoping when I was back in the USA to meet Tony in person at

The beauty and majesty of the Himalaya Mountains

a retreat he was giving in Los Angeles, California. Unfortunately Tony died of a heart attack in New York on his way to California. Hal and Sidra were offering one of their annual Summer Camps in the L.A. area at the time. So they invited me to join them since my arrangements had been made to travel to L.A. I joined their staff as a good substitute for the retreat. The other thing I want to mention is I met Laurence Freeman, OSB in Mumbai. Laurence is John Main's successor in teaching Christian Meditation. It was this meeting that put me on a committed path to daily mantra, breath and walking meditation taught by John Main and also taught by Thich Nhat Hanh.

Father Joe and I parted as friends and I would return. This temporarily ended my visit to India but opened up other doors as usually happens. It is my experience that when one door closes another opens if we stay awake and are ready. I was.

Me finishing presiding at my retirement liturgy.

CHAPTER FOURTEEN

Back home to the USA
Church of St. Mary of the Lake
1996-1999

Back to my roots

After my two years in India with Kripa, I was back home to the Archdiocese of St. Paul and Minneapolis and Minnesota. I was back to my roots. I was blessed to have a Pastor friend, Father Roger Pierre at St. Mary of the Lake in White Bear Lake. Roger provided a home for me in the parish rectory connected to the church. Thirty years ago Fr. Roger came to St. Pius X in White Bear Lake and became my associate pastor. Now at St. Mary's in White Bear Lake, I became his associate pastor. This was a welcome change for me. I enjoyed my time at St. Mary of the Lake and I was there from 1996 to 1999. When I arrived at age 65, I could retire from active ministry in the Archdiocese. This would free me from local responsibilities along with some added income to serve in the Third World. I felt I had made my contribution to the local church. We are so blessed in the United States of America with so much and the Third World has so little. My commitment was to pay my own way to different parts of the Third World. The places I served at offered to take care of my room and board. I had two simple requirements: 1. Water to drink that was safe. 2. A western toilet since I was not adept at squatting as many in the Third World do so easily. I did not expect a stipend for my services. I would receive one on occasion. This may sound strange, but with this arrangement I could live cheaper out of the country in the Third World than here in the USA.

As a young priest with a limited income, I was told to plan to have some investments to help me after I was no longer in active ministry in the Archdiocese. I did this and along with this I chose to live a simple lifestyle. This arrangement worked in the past and works out well for me even today. We receive a reasonable pension from

Jan, Gloria and Terri - three women friends provided hospitality for my retirement celebration.

SEPTEMBER 9, 1999

RETIREMENT

St. Mary of the Lake in White Bear Lake to celebrate the 65th birthday and retirement of Father Whittier

St. Mary of the Lake in White Bear Lake will celebrate the retirement and 65th birthday of Father William Whittier during the weekend of Sept. 25 and 26.

A reception is planned after the 5 p.m. Mass on Saturday, Sept. 25, and after the 7:30, 9 and 11 a.m. Masses on Sunday, Sept. 26. It will continue until 2 p.m. on Sunday. Father Whittier will preside at the Saturday Mass and preach at all the weekend Masses at St. Mary, 4690 Bald Eagle Avenue.

Father Whittier was ordained

Father Whittier

for the Archdiocese of St. Paul and Minneapolis in 1961.

Since that time he has served the archdiocese as an associate pastor or pastor at Maternity of Mary in St. Paul; St. Matthew in West St. Paul; St. Pius X in White Bear Lake; St.

Edward in Bloomington; St. Bridget of Sweden in Lindstrom and Immaculate Conception in Columbia Heights.

He also has served at St. Mary Magdalen in Los Angeles and at Mount Carmel in Mambai, India.

For many years, Father Whittier served as a consultant at Hazelden Renewal Center in Center City.

He plans to continue his teaching and service to Third World countries.

the Archdiocese and this I would get at age 65. I do not like to use the word retirement and my mentor and friend Hal Stone says we should remove it from our vocabulary. I agree since it labels people in a way that is not accurate. It also limits possibilities in one's own mind and in the mind of others. I like the word "refired" rather than "retired." We are refired by the Spirit of the Living God of the Universe to continue new challenges in our journey of life. During this time of going back to my roots in White Bear Lake, Minnesota, more possibilities opened up for me for serving in the Third World. Through a priest friend who lived with me at the time at St. Mary of the Lake, I met Sister Josefina from Manila and Assumption College in the Philippines. With my teaching of the Psychology of the *Aware Ego* and *Voice Dialogue*, she invited me to come to Assumption College for part of the year. I would offer the teaching to the Sisters in the Communities there and to the faculty at Assumption College. So my priesthood and background in the Psychology of *Aware Ego* and *Voice Dialogue* worked together to bring me to the Philippines. I have continued to make visits back there the last few years. I met Aris through relationships at Assumption College. Aris was then a seminarian on leave teaching in one of their schools. Aris is now a priest who I have helped in different ways along his life journey. We continue to be dear friends. His full family name is Aristotle Miranda Maniago. He is now on the faculty of the Catholic University in San Fernando. Not long ago via Skype, he called out for help. He was in Japan and lonely and at a loss to speak their

My sister Charlotte and brothers John and Larry celebrating with me my "refiring" liturgy.

language. Just our contact helped relieve him of some of his loneliness. He was planning to come visit me this summer, but this got postponed to next summer, Inshallah.

Mark Bompat was the computer "fixer" at the College. We became close friends. At a young age he lost both his father and mother by death. He was parentless, so I offered to be his father; so I became his dad. Another self got named, "Dad." Not long ago the phone rang here in New Hope and the voice on the other end said, "Hi dad." I paused not knowing who it was. Mark then said, "Dad don't you remember me? This is your son Mark." Mark called to let his "dad" know he was married a year ago and now he was a father. This made me a grandfather. Sending pictures via the internet I could see that his wife is beautiful and his son as well. I had never seen Mark looking so happy. So my international family grows in different ways and this makes me happy and grateful. The only trouble is all my family is so far away.

My background in the AA Recovery program learned at Hazelden came in here as well. I met while at Assumption (but not in Assumption) many persons involved in recovery. These relationships opened another whole area for me to be involved in. Gaye affectionately known as "the pleaser," Dondi and Bernie who all are involved in rehabs became my great friends

Other relatives that came to celebrate with me my "refiring" liturgy.

in recovery. These friendships still exist. Gaye gave himself the name "the pleaser." He discovered with *Voice Dialogue* how his pleaser played a very significant part in his multiple addictions. The Assumption Sisters had communities in a number of the Islands, so I traveled there to offer them the teaching. I was well received as well as the teaching. The Sisters were very good to me and I to them. Since that year my involvement has been more with the persons in Recovery. These persons and organizations were all working to call alcoholics and addicts back to life from their disease of addiction. There is so much education needed, not only in the Manila area but still in the USA and other parts of the world. The education is around the disease concept of addiction. PERSONS LIVING WITH ALCOHOLISM ARE NOT BAD PEOPLE WHO NEED PUNISHMENT BUT SICK PEOPLE WHO NEED HEALING. This cannot be repeated enough times around the world. There are more jails filled with alcoholics than rehabs in the Philippines.

I have been blessed in so many ways and affirmed in what I am doing by friends and also by Hal and Sidra Stone. Hal and Sidra send me free books and other needed educational material of their teachings. My more recent connection with Jody Klescewski at Hazelden provides free Hazelden publications for my needs in recovery work in the Third World. The one downside is many of the people I serve and work with do not know English. As you might suspect most the educational materials are

Sisters of the Assumption were delighted with my presence and teaching.

not in the languages of the countries I visit but in English. I encourage people and countries I serve to honor and keep their own language and culture but also to learn English. I see English becoming more and more the universal language on our planet. If more people had the opportunity to learn English, this would save a lot of need for translations and the costs involved. Having a common language also could possibly bring us together as one Family of God. Maybe someday?

Phoenix is a Therapeutic Community for the rehabilitation of substance dependents. It is located in Tagaytay. The President is my friend Bernie Termulo. When teaching and counseling there I would stay at the Divine Word Seminary close by which is in and surrounded by beautiful gardens.

CHAPTER FIFTEEN

A Reflection From The Philippines 2001-2002

"Life is a journey to find ourselves, our own wisdom and our God."

I t seems to me when we find one of the above we find all three, but the journey goes on with infinite expansion of consciousness. I write this chapter in Tagaytay, the tourist haven west of Manila. Tagaytay is in the mountains where it is so much cooler than hot and humid Manila. In many ways having given some hints about understanding the process of the *Aware Ego*, I would see the journey of life could be called the journey of the *Aware Ego*—ever expanding and balancing the opposites in our lives.

I have reflected on my visit to India with some brief indication of how life went for me there. In this chapter I am going to put together some of the ideas and convictions I have at this stage in my life journey. Both Hal Stone and Bede Griffiths put out the message to not abandon your roots but build on them. I have honored this and other mentors like Thich Nhat Hanh, Gandhi, Mother Teresa, John Henry Newman, Chardin, Bill W. (the founder of AA), John Main, and Jesus in the Gospel have all suggested the same. We need to stay grounded in our roots. Then we expand and grow from there. The caution is to not get stuck like a rock in the river of life. Keep moving with the river of life.

I feel this has been true for me. I am a small town boy grown up to be a Catholic Priest, World Counselor and Teacher, still honoring my roots as an American and a Catholic Christian.

What I have learned I practice the best I know how. This learning is to live in the present moment where life, recovery, grace and God are. Life is an evolutionary process which takes courage and the pushing of boundaries to keep alive. Spirituality calls us to find our God and be connected in love. This makes an important distinction between religion and spirituality as is clarified by Bill W. in the 12 Steps of AA. I have found that the 12 Steps of AA embody the essence of all the world religions when we move beyond the surface of rules and laws and rituals and meet in the cave of the heart. Thomas Merton in *Contemplative Prayer* described the cave of the heart in this way. "It refers to the deepest psychological ground of one's personality, the inner sanctuary where self-awareness goes beyond analytical reflection and opens out into metaphysical and theological confrontation with the Abyss of the unknown yet present— one who is more intimate to us than we are to ourselves."

We are called to learn from our Eastern Brothers and Sisters as Bede

Griffiths has modeled so well. We need an *Aware Ego* who will hold and honor the balance and tension between what is of lasting value in the wedding of both.

As I have studied and followed my mentors, I have found that the mystery and message of the Gospel of Jesus becomes more clear. It becomes for me more alive, more challenging and more relevant.

As I have traveled around our home planet earth, I have discovered that human nature and all its needs and longings and diseases are the same. They are the same but they all have a little different cultural touch or taste. The 12 Steps of AA have a common ground all over the world. They are free from all the religious differences that are surface and separate people, countries and even families from each other. Meditation or Contemplation invites us and empowers us to go beyond the surface and find the God of our Understanding. This is the same God of all world religions, dwelling in the cave of our heart.

I see that the Catholic Church and all the World Religions and my home, this United States of America, need to take up this invitation. We need to honor our roots but also be clear about what is essential and foundational and expand from there. America keeps struggling to be true to the Constitution of our Founding Fathers and Mothers. Christianity has accumulated much in terms of human laws and rituals which needs to be reevaluated in the light of Jesus Christ and the message of the Gospel. Other World Religions need to go back to their roots to be faithful to what is essential to enable them to have vital and solid spirituality.

This is the challenge before us as individuals, countries and our home planet earth. As we hear so often, it is easy to talk the talk, but so difficult and challenging to walk the talk, be it Christianity, other world religions, Recovery or the Constitution of the USA. Let us accept the challenge and walk the talk.

Tabor Lodge in Cork Ireland prior to its new addition

CHAPTER SIXTEEN

Relationship as Teacher
2003

One of the teachings I learned from Hal and Sidra Stone is "relationship as teacher." One closely related to this one also from them is "illness as teacher." They both fit with the work I have done and am doing. This is the work both with the Psychology of the *Aware Ego* and *Voice Dialogue* and the rehabilitation of persons living with alcoholism and other addictions.

Sister Margaret, Fr. Vincent and Sister Rose, Founders of Tabor Lodge.

"Active addicts don't have relationships; they take hostages." This is a word of wisdom from 12 Step work.

I pinpoint at the beginning of this chapter "relationship as teacher," since so much of my life journey has come about and been enhanced by relationship both as teacher, but also as connector with persons. Sometimes I am a slow learner from relationships. Since I am not in a primary relationship like marriage, I miss the learning that is available in this relationship. I would like now to insert one of my favorite and daily prayers by my mentor John Henry Cardinal Newman. This speaks to me about relationship as connection and also about God being in charge.

> "God has created me to do Him some definite service. He has committed some work to me which he has not committed to another. I have my mission. I may never know it in this life, but I shall be told it in the next.
>
> I am a link in a chain, a bond of connection between persons. He has not created me for naught. I shall do well. I shall do His work. I shall be an angel of peace, a preacher of truth in my own place

while not intending it, if I but keep His commandments.

Therefore, I will trust Him. Whatever, wherever I am I can never be thrown away. If I am sickness, my sickness may serve Him; in perplexity, my perplexity may serve Him; if I am in sorrow, my sorrow may serve Him. He does nothing in vain. He knows what He is about. He may take away my friends. He may throw me among strangers. He may make me feel desolate, make my spirits sink, hide my future from me, still He knows what He is about."

I have found this prayer so true to my experience of my life journey. So many of my connections around the world have been by relationships. I do not go where I do not have relationships. Often I am there because of a relationship made elsewhere.

Brige and John Hill and me

I met Brige and John Hill in Nigeria with my first visit there and Brige was in recovery. At that time she and John were helping support Our Lady of Victory Rehab center. This is the rehab center outside of Jos, Nigeria, I helped Fr. Jacob found. She related well to the *Voice Dialogue* experience I offered her at that time. She and John then moved with John's work to South Africa. They became my connection with South Africa. Through workshops sponsored by Brige, in Johannesburg, came the connection with Nellie, Ethne and the Centering Prayer communities. Nellie connected me with Leslie Zimmerman, a Jungian analyst who found new insights and help with her work from the Psychology of *Aware Ego* and *Voice Dialogue*. So this planted the seeds of the work in South Africa and got me there. We plant and let God call to life and nurture and bring to full growth, and God does.

Through Planet aide in Minneapolis I met Dr. Chris from Faith Alive Clinic in Jos, Nigeria. Dr. Chris was my connection with Faith Alive Clinic and back with Jos, Nigeria. This was a reconnecting with relationships made back when Our Lady of Victory Rehab was born in the same area of Jos, Nigeria.

Entrance to Tabor Lodge, Cork, Ireland.

Tabor Lodge in Cork, Ireland, was my relationship with Sister Margaret and her staff who came to train at Hazelden. Some of her staff lived with me back when I was pastor at St. Bridget of Sweden. Tabor Lodge in Cork, Ireland, was a wonderful stopping off place for me as I came from Mumbai to Amsterdam. I would take a break in my flight at Amsterdam and go off to Cork for a week or more before flying home to Minneapolis.

Then at Tabor Lodge I met Denis, a recovering addict. Denis was doing work in education and addiction in Kenya. He was looking for someone else to come and help him. At the recommendation of Mick Devine the then-director of Tabor Lodge, I said yes to Denis. Before I said yes to Denis he assured me that my two requirements would be met as I suggested before. Again this was relationship. This commitment was for about a month two years in a row along with commitments still in South Africa, Jos, Nigeria, and Kripa in India. Then came my meeting with Pete and Fr. Sam from Uganda and the need to strengthen AA and Rehab work there. Fr. Sam invited me to come to Uganda and help him. Again here is a connecting relationship. I said yes to Fr. Sam's invitation and will discuss further in the chapter on Uganda. Another relationship is my living situation in New Hope, Minnesota. I met Helen Fagerberg 30 years ago as she shared her wisdom through Bible Teaching at St. Pius X in White Bear Lake, Minnesota. Our relationship and friendship continued. Then I met her daughter Sonja who lived and taught and wrote books for the natives in Senegal. Sonja's mother Helen died suddenly in her condo in New Hope and Sonja became the owner. Sonja then invited me to live and

Helen Fagerberg

care for the furnished condo paying the maintenance costs. This was a blessing for me with all my traveling. It was a very financially reasonable and furnished place for me to call home. Along with this I have an underground heated garage and lovely people to live with. Then Sonja died suddenly in Senegal. Now her son Yacine will own the condo. Hopefully when things get settled, I will continue the same arrangement with him as I had with his mother. My meeting the challenge to write this autobiography has connected me with David Gawlik from Caritas Communications. In some of the other chapters I have alluded to other relationships not mentioned here.

CHAPTER SEVENTEEN

The Roar of Awakening
2003

"The Roar of Awakening" is a story from West Bengal in India found in Hal and Sidra's first book, *Embracing Ourselves*. I cite this story because it is the story I always use to introduce the Psychology of *Aware Ego* and *Voice Dialogue*. This can be at a rehab or in other settings for teaching like at Assumption College in Manila. I will share the story and then explain its meaning and how I use it in enhancing my teaching. It is the story of each one of us as we make our journey of life here on our home planet, earth.

One day a female tiger who was carrying her baby in her tummy was wandering around the jungle and savannah looking for food. She was extra hungry since she was feeding two people, herself, and her baby. She came upon a herd of goats and since tigers are meat eating she attacked the herd of goats. She killed some and the others ran away for safety. Goats are like people, they are nosey. So the goats who survived came sneaking back peeking around the bushes to see what happened to their

fellow goats and the mother tiger. As they peered around the bushes they saw some of their fellow goats dead and they were sad at the sight. However to their surprise they saw the mother tiger lying there dead but with her little cub beside her very much alive. The energy it took to attack the goats

killed the mother tiger. Before she died she brought forth her very much alive baby cub. So with this the goats who survived were faced with a decision. What should they do about the baby tiger? At this point in the story I ask my audience what they think the goats should do. Some respond, "Adopt the baby." Some respond, "Kill the baby." Others suggest, "Leave it there to die." The goats like most of us love a baby so they decided to adopt the tiger. The baby tiger went off with the goats and grew up in their care. The tiger as it got bigger and bigger physically became more and more internally like a goat. It smelled like a goat. It became vegetarian like a goat and it would "ba ba" like a goat. Then one day a large male tiger came by looking for food. He spotted the herd of goats but also the young tiger that was quite large by this time. The male tiger was very puzzled how this tiger got with the goats. He said to himself, "Doesn't that tiger know who he is?" Being hungry he let this question pass and filled his hungry tummy with goat meat. Having finished eating, the large male tiger turned around. To his surprise the young tiger did not run away with the goats. So down deep inside this young tiger, made goat, knew he did not have to be afraid. He did not run away. The challenge now of the male tiger was how to wake up this tiger, become goat. He wanted him to realize he is a tiger and not a goat. At this point to add some drama and humor to the story I invite someone from the audience to help me. I then with some drama go through the process of waking the young tiger up. First we look into a pool of water serving as mirror to see if the young tiger realizes he is a handsome tiger like me and wakes up. He does not wake up. I smell him and get him to "ba ba" like a goat. I try a second time to wake him up and this time stuffing some goat meat down his throat. In doing this I hope it will reach his tummy. When it does he will realize he is carnivorous and wake up to who he is. But he just throws the meat up and still "ba ba" like a goat and smells like a goat. I mention I travel to USA and know the national sport of baseball and there are three strikes and out. So I suggest we try one more time to wake him up. If he does not respond I will let him wander around the planet not knowing who he is. What to use this time to wake him up? Some wise guys at this point suggest I bring in a female tiger. She would wake him up. I could not find a female tiger. There is some goat blood left. I will see if that will reach his tummy and wake him up. I put some down his throat and it goes to his tummy. He wakes up with a roar of awakening and I invite him to roar. I acknowledge he must come with me to the jungle because he needs to learn a lot about how to be a tiger. At this point I recognize the person who helped me. We give him a round of applause and I give him a hug of thanks.

I invite the audience to see how this is the story of each one of us as we go from a vulnerable baby like the tiger to adulthood. At this point I explain how we by our family system, education, and culture, different forms of abuse and drugs and alcohol can get lost on our life journey. We no longer know who we are. In the language of the story we become goats. God, who is in some way represented by the big male tiger in the story, wants each of us to wake up to find who we are and to be ourselves. To make this happen God sends wake up times into our lives to wake us up. These can be in the form of health issues, death of a loved one, divorce if married, a powerful dream, falling in love. Maybe because of drugs and alcohol we are put out of the house or in a rehab or both and these and other examples can be wake up times. The audience usually gets what I mean and if in a rehab environment, it is the rehab that helps them wake up and find themselves and be themselves.

From this I move into explaining how we became goats, by using the psycho-spiritual language of the Psychology of *Aware Ego* and *Voice Dialogue*. I provide two diagrams to help them. I put the diagrams on the board as well and explain what they mean. At the end of this chapter I will include the diagrams I give to them as teaching aids.

How we became goats is the teaching metaphor I use. The circle with the VC in the diagram is our vulnerable child. The three arrows point up why this child who is in each one of us is so important. The vulnerable child carries our psychic fingerprint, our emotions, feelings, and our vulnerability and is the spiritual doorway of our soul to God. A small heart in the child is a symbol of God's love poured forth in our hearts by the Holy Spirit. Or as the Hindus would put it, the God of the Universe loving us in silence in the cave of our heart. This points to the Eastern way of Spirituality of meditation and contemplation. I have another arrow pointing to God who is also outside of the child and represents the God of transcendence. The God who lives in the whole universe and transcends it. This is more the Western way of Spirituality. The point I am making is to show how important this child is and how we lose touch with it as we become goats. I then go into explaining five Primary Selves which I see are the big ones. As we journey through life, the Primary Selves circle around the vulnerable child, eventually making us lose touch with our child and all the child stands for. Thus we become goats. The selves I choose to encircle the Vulnerable Child are Pleaser, Pusher, Perfectionist, Critic, and Rational Mind. They are not bad or good but can be too small or too big. They can throw our life out of balance and can be the cause of addiction or other health or growth issues. In order to not go too long, I will not go into all the detail here. Rehabs are often full of big pleasers who do not know how to say no and set boundaries. Since they experience not being loved, or feelings of anger or frustration, drugs find their way into their lives. Perfectionists are frustrated in not being perfect so find relief by getting into drugs. Pushers do not know how to relax naturally so use drugs and alcohol to relax. We turn a big critic off by escape into drugs and alcohol or other addictions. Rational Minds suppress feelings and these feelings get out when our minds are not in control. Our minds are not in control when involved with drugs and alcohol. So wake up times come in many ways and we develop an *Aware Ego* and enter into the process of Recovery. We recognize our Primary selves and own the disowned opposite selves from these primary selves. We learn to say no and set boundaries. We can be beach bums and relax without drugs. We do not have to be perfect and we can allow mistakes and imperfection in ourselves and others. In separating from our critic, we learn how to affirm ourselves and move out of judgment. We separate from our rational mind with the opposite of expressing our feelings and emotions and intuition. As we do this separation we are developing an *Aware Ego* between these opposites. In this balance and tension of opposites is where the process of Recovery happens. This is the challenge of life and growth. This process of holding the opposite energies is the ongoing challenge of our life journey and growth in an *Aware Ego*. I have simplified, but I hope this is helpful. For more understanding I recommend the books and DVD's of Hal and Sidra Stone. I then give a demonstration of *Voice Dialogue* to let them see how these selves can be talked to and their different energies sensed. From this the balance of opposites is facilitated. After the demonstration I invite those interested in pursuing the *Voice Dialogue* process to contact me for a more private session. Some choose to do so and some do not.

PSYCHOLOGY OF THE AWARE EGO

PROCESS: VOICE DIALOGUE

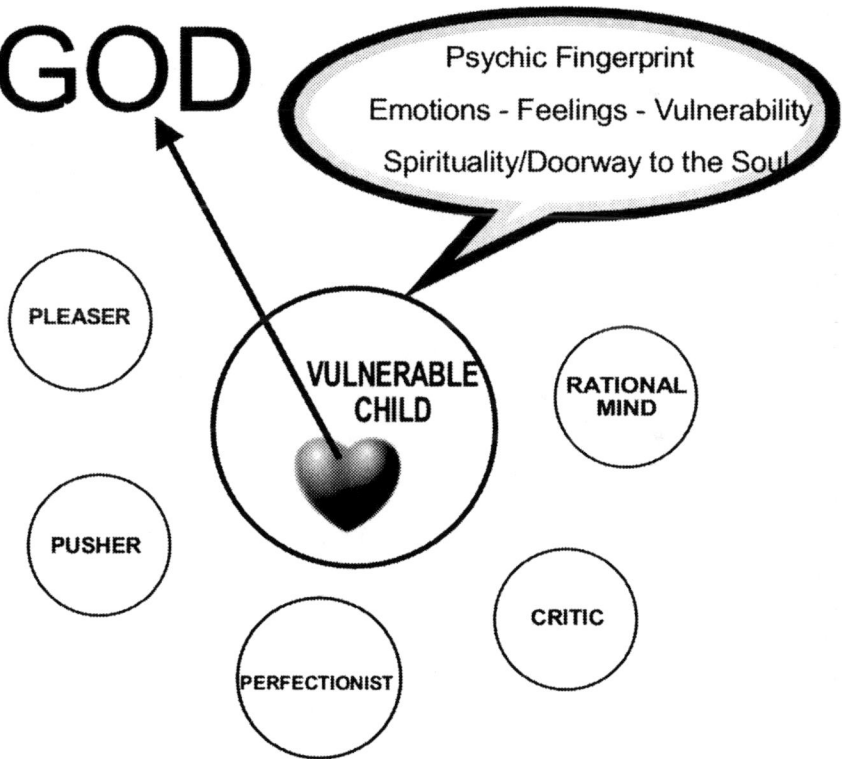

These primary selves protect the child but also block access to the child.

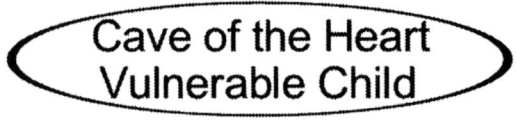

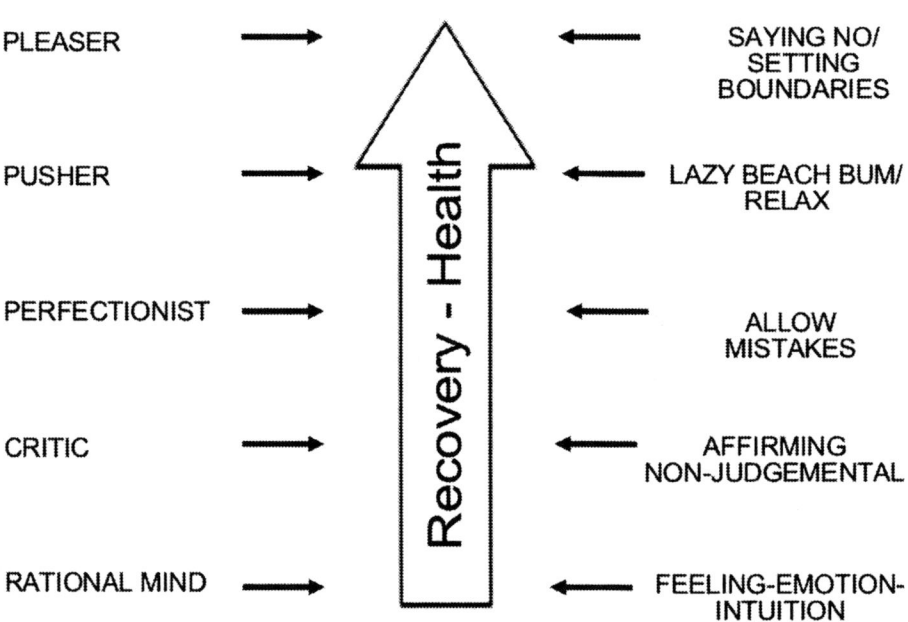

AWARE EGO
Embraces opposites and provides choice

Ujjal and his wife Rimpa and son Utsav

CHAPTER EIGHTEEN

Bagdogra
2004

When I first came to Kripa I heard Ossie, who was the Center Manager of Kripa Bandra at the time, mention Bagdogra. What is Bagdogra? Where is it? It seemed a strange name to me. Then I found out it is a small city that you need to fly into to have access to Darjeeling and Sikkim. Neither of these areas have direct air access. Bagdogra is on the plains and from there you need to take a vehicle like a jeep or van or bus to climb up the steep road to Darjeeling and not so steep road to Sikkim. From Darjeeling there is the historical toy train which partially functions today. This was the train Mother Teresa was travelling on coming down from Darjeeling when she got a message from God. The message was to leave her present religious order and serve the poor.

kc, a recovering addict I met in Kripa Darjeeling and was director of Sikkim Rehabe in Gangtok where Ujjal and I taught

Bagdogra has become a favorite place for me to visit. In the more recent past I have not taken the rather steep and somewhat scary ride up to Darjeeling. If you tend to have anxiety attacks or the like I would suggest you stay in Bagdogra. Bishop Thomas is the Bishop there and I first met him in my early visits to Darjeeling. He was the Administrator of the Diocese of Darjeeling until Bishop Stephen was installed. Bishop Thomas always gave me hospitality at the Good Shepherd Church which is also the Cathedral Church for Bagdogra. The church has a very convenient location very near the airport. Just since my traveling there, the airport has been renovated. It has expanded to be a first class airport and maybe now an International Airport. Marina is there in Bagdogra. Marina is the motel started by Grandpa Edwards who I knew well. I visited him often before he died. His son Bonnie is now in charge of Marina along with his son Rajiv. They have expanded the motel (like the airport has expanded) to meet the needs of more travelers needing overnight accommodations. I am welcomed also to stay at their motel as well. On one of my first visits to Bagdogra I met in one of the local shops a wonderful and gifted young man named Ujjal. We became almost instant friends. I challenged him to move out of the shop and go back to school which was the desire of his mother but not his father who ran the shop. His father had two wives and Ujjal and his mother lived in the same house with the second wife and a son born of her. As Ujjal and I were becoming friends his mother became seriously ill and died. With her death we became even closer friends. He was interested in my teachings on the Psychology of *Aware Ego* and Voice Ego. I helped him get a computer to expand his horizon some more. This education expansion was the dream of his mother for Ujjal. Today he is married and has a lovely wife Rimpa and a son Utsav. He travels with me when I go to Sikkim since he is street smart and knows the drivers of the jeeps. When we need a jeep to travel to Sikkim I stay out of sight. This way I am not seen and he gets a better fare. He also makes sure we get the front seat of the jeep for my comfort. I could never handle this all alone. So he has become my traveling companion when I have gone a number

Bonnie Edwards and his wife Cecilia and Grandpa Edwards in the middle

of times to Sikkim. We visit a rehab there run by a recovering addict from Kripa Darjeeling. We together have taught the Psychology of the *Aware Ego* and *Voice Dialogue* to clients in the rehab. He has served as a good translator. I need him with my language limitation of only English. So the mysterious Bagdogra has become a wonderful home when I travel there. Ujjal calls me Papa and I am honored. We jog together and "kick each other in the ass" figuratively if either of us needs a good reminder of something.

Grandpa Edwards and his son Bonnie's large family also have Glenary's up in Darjeeling. This is a lovely bakery, restaurant and cyber café. This provides another home for me when I have stayed at the Bishop's House. I am offered good meals and hospitality with their family. The bakery is also a cyber café. They offer me free access to send and receive email. As I travel as Fr. Gulliver, email has been and is my life line to family and friends around the world.

So briefly this is what the mysterious Bagdogra has come to mean for me. It is like many of the Kripa centers—a welcoming home away from home.

Imphal Kripa staff at a meeting in Calcutta

CHAPTER NINETEEN

Tribals From Nagaland, Manipur And Darjeeling 2005

When I first came to Kripa, I met in Kripa Bandra young men and women from Nagaland, Manipur and Darjeeling. They were there because at this time Kripa did not have rehabs in their respective areas. They were referred to as tribals. I sensed in some ways they were looked down upon by some of the clients from Mumbai and the city. But I was attracted to them by their ability to speak good English, since this was my native language and the only language I knew. To me they knew better English than some of the clients from the city like Mumbai. I found them very bright as well. They reminded me of our tribals in the USA, the Native Americans. They were more in touch with nature and with their bodies. They were simple in the best sense of the word. They loved to sing and dance because of this living close to nature and their bodies. I love nature myself and nature nourishes my Spirituality. Maybe this was another reason for my attraction to them. I understood the Baptist Missionaries had come in to the Northeast early and brought Christianity and the English language. This was my initial introduction and a favorable one to these tribals from the Northeast. I would include Darjeeling with them.

Since my initial visit to Kripa, Kripa has extended rehabs to these areas. This provided an opportunity for me to meet the tribals in their local environment. I have mentioned my visits to Darjeeling earlier in my writing. In making my visits to Kripa rehabs I wanted to visit Nagaland and Manipur as well. They presented another challenge for me. They were protected areas and insurgent attacks were common. As a foreigner I needed to have a special permit to enter. The insurgents do not attack outsiders or foreigners. They primarily were fighting the Indian Government and the Indian Army. These permits were for a limited time and for a limited area in these States. I made one visit to Nagaland through the help of Bonnie Edward's brother who lived there and had a school there. One of Bonnie's nephews took me on a grand tour of Nagaland. I even traveled with some of the insurgents. They slept in the same room with me with their guns under their pillows. But I felt safe and taken care of. This was one of the few times I was having stomach problems. To my embarrassment and discomfort, we had to stop often for me to clean out my stomach. This was the downside of this trip, but I and they hung in there. Yes, I was well taken care of. As we traveled around together I experienced the tribal living and also the beautiful natural settings. I could see if they could settle their insurgent disputes they could develop a wonderful tourist area. This could bring much needed income into their state and help build their infrastructure. I was disappointed in that I did not meet any of the Naga boys I first met in Kripa Bandra. But I visited the Kripa Rehab Center where many young men were dealing with their addiction. Many were even injecting into their legs. In doing this their legs became extremely infected. They were not a pretty sight. Drugs, and mainly the pure form of Heroin, are so prevalent coming from the erstwhile "Golden Triangle" in Myanmar (Burma). Young people both men and women get into using drugs due to their genetic propensity to become addicted. Their addiction also comes from their family system issues and other environmental factors. It broke my heart to see the damage done to these beautiful young people. Parents were burying their young sons and daughters rather than the usual practice of children burying their aged parents. Because the mode of drug intake was primarily through injection, many were sharing their needles and syringes. This resulted in many

Teaching in Kripa Imphal

of them living with HIV and some dying of AIDS. This was my one and only visit to Nagaland and the one visit was sufficient for me.

Manipur their neighbor was into the same issues. I needed a permit as well to enter Manipur. I often would confuse Manipur which is the State with Imphal which is the Capital of Manipur. Imphal is the city where Kripa has a rehab. The rehab is very small and needs much attention to improve its facilities. A new facility is on the drawing board and land is available. I am not sure when it will become a reality. I have visited Imphal much more often than Nagaland since access is easier for me and the permit easier to obtain. Another plus for my more frequent visits is that the Archbishop's House is close by Kripa. I am always welcome to stay there when I visit. The physical comfort provided meets my needs and the hospitality of the Archbishop and the priests is extraordinary.

Some of the Imphal Staff on a Street in Calcutta drinking tea with me while waiting to meet Mother Teresa

The infrastructure of Imphal is very poor. The phone lines are often not available. Road construction is ongoing and slow. This makes for dusty, bumpy and dirty travelling not only for me but for the locals. One thing that amazed me was all the bicycle rickshaws. Their drivers are young men who have no other opportunity for work. Many are well educated I am told. I marveled at the headlights on the rickshaws. I had to see one at night to believe it. The headlight is a tin can with top and bottom removed and a candle inserted in the center of the can. Not much light but they served the purpose when no other kind of headlights are available.

As in Nagaland armed conflict was always ongoing. I was very limited to where I could travel, and night travel was not allowed. I was always instructed during the day to never travel alone lest I be abducted and held for ransom but not harmed. If abducted I am not sure how much ransom I would be worth or who would pay it. I myself felt safe there and the limits of the permit sort of cramped my style. I am a high sensation person and I always want to explore and see all I could. Like a little kid I would often go where angels would fear to tread. Again this is an indication of the gift I have of a very high trust level.

Anand and me

In the earlier days, Anand was the Center Manager of Kripa Imphal. We first met in Mumbai at Kripa Bandra. I remember we had some serious discussion about his desire to marry and he being HIV positive. My suggestion was that he makes sure his wife-to-be knows he was HIV positive like so many other young men there. It was also very important that he explain the danger for her and any possible children becoming infected. He understood. He did get married and he was blessed that neither his wife nor his two lovely children are infected. Anand and I have become very dear friends over these years. He moved on from Kripa to the staff of Catholic Relief Services based in Guwahati. Anand has a deep love for the people in Imphal and so many there are living with HIV and or AIDS. From our visits I would say Mother Teresa is his inspiration as well. There are many widows and children left at the death of their husbands and fathers. They need lots of help. Anand, through his work with CRS and working with Kripa Imphal, has been providing much needed help. He sees the need for even more help. With his and my friend Gopen they have inspired me to set up an AIDS Care Foundation though the IRS in the USA. If we could set it up this would provide even more help to the people there.

When I first wrote this I and Michael Santori, a good friend dating back to St. Matthew's and an excellent Chiropractor, were in the process of getting the USA IRS Office to approve the AIDS Care Foundation. If we got approval and are tax exempt we hoped to access grant money for additional help. This help would be primarily for Imphal and others in similar need. This accessing grant money would be another challenge for us if and when ACF gets IRS approval. We continued to pursue this approval. Mike and his wife Karen did much of the work since I was out of the country. As we made progress (or so we thought), we discovered the red tape just got to be overwhelming. So Mike at my suggestion wrote a letter to thank them saying the red tape overwhelmed us. We decided not to pursue this approval any further. In many ways this is a relief for us. If we got approval this would be another tremendous challenge to access grant money and all the other detail that goes with this. At this time in my life I am not very excited about trying to access money.

But my interest in Imphal and helping them goes back to the soft spot in my heart for these tribals beginning when I first came to Kripa Bandra. I confess my soft spot grows and gets bigger as I continue with my visits to Imphal and nurture my ongoing love and friendship with Anand. Anand is scheduled for a visit to the CRS headquarters in Baltimore in September. A visit to Minnesota to see me is on the itinerary.

Anand did arrive at my home and I provided hospitality for him. He was scheduled to speak at the University of St. Thomas my alma mater of 50 years ago. I had not been back recently to St. Thomas and I offered to accompany him and help in any way I could. I enjoyed having him with me and enjoyed hearing his presentation, which was a good one. I also enjoyed his presence in my home. He on the floor with his computer and at the desk with mine working and enjoying our presence together. I am blessed to have him as a friend. His visit may even get me somewhat involved with CRS; Inshallah (God Willing).He made an ideal person to host because he is an "*aware ego* perfectionist" and takes good care of himself and his surroundings. When he left all was in order and maybe in better order than when he came. Thanks Anand for your visit and come again.

Small group session in my teaching of *Voice Dialogue* in Kripa Imphal.

Another contact and friend in Imphal who I need to mention is Father Francis who heads up the Catholic Medical Center. Along with Fr. Francis I need also to mention the Sisters who staff the Medical Center along with their dedicated staff. They were a big help to me in attempting to have the infection I picked up in Goa to say goodbye to my body. We tried, and with some pain, but the infection refused to say goodbye at this time. It followed me to Ireland. My relationship with them and their hospitality is another reason why Imphal gets a regular visit by me when I am in India.

Fr. Bill and Dr. Chris dancing at the Persons' living with AIDS support group at Faith Alive Clinic after being "refired."

CHAPTER TWENTY

Nigeria, South Africa and Kenya
2006-2007

After being "refired" with the Spirit of the Living God, some other doors of service opened up in Jos, Nigeria, Johannesburg in South Africa, and extending to Kenya, and even to Uganda. I am now typing this chapter on January 2, 2009, in Gulu, Northern Uganda. Again as I mentioned in an earlier writing these connections all came about through relationships. Jos, Nigeria this time came about with my relationship with Dr. Chris who I met in Minneapolis Dr. Chris is a very gifted doctor and University Professor. He has had many an offer for a good position in USA but chose to stay to help his own people through the Faith Alive Free Clinic. Dr. Chris always insists the Clinic is free even though some with money take advantage of the service. Young student doctors volunteer their services there and the care is excellent. His wife Mercy is a surgeon and they both amaze me in their generosity in serving their own people and raising their family in Nigeria. In December, Dr. Chris was abducted, stripped naked and left tied up in the bush. His money and car were stolen. He got himself untied and returned home unharmed. Later he found his car in Cameroon and two of the thugs were caught. One of my pet peeves is gifted people from Africa and other Third World countries leaving their own people who need their expertise to take positions in the USA or other western countries. But I realize in these countries job opportunities, money and comfort far exceed what they have in their home country. In some ways I feel like the "odd ball" coming from the USA to serve and help them rather than stay home with all the comfort available there. This is God's doing not mine. I have no regrets and God has been super good to me. Actually after being "refired" these experiences have just kept the fire glowing and blazing at times. My sense is my homeland of USA has many retired gifted people who could allow God to "refire" them. They could make a real contribution to bringing their many professional and personal gifts to serve in the Third World. But this is their choice and their openness to be "refired" by the Spirit of the Living God of all the World Religions.

My return to join Dr. Chris in Jos, Nigeria, was where I first came by the invitation of Father Jacob. My return reconnected me with many friends I had made back in those early days in Jos. There have been the brothers Peter and Joseph Gotau and their families. Joseph now is establishing an organization to help some of the extremely poor in Nigeria. I hope to be of some help to him in this project. Stephen Dauda has finished University and is in local politics. I call him with his education and dedication

Stephen Dauda

"the Obama of Jos." Along the way I have helped him with his education. I met Simon, and I have become to him his "Soul Lifter" and "Kaka," which is grandfather in their local language. Here are some more selves named for me. I have encouraged Simon and helped him in some limited ways with starting a business and getting more schooling. He keeps telling me and I know he means it. He wants to help make a little better world like he sees me doing. Simon along with some of the staff at the Clinic are some of the new friends I have made in Jos. I am amazed with what little material comfort so many of the people have here in Jos, Nigeria. Yet they live, raise families and are happy. When I do my morning walk they are out smiling and greeting me and opening their little shops along the road. You see firsthand what their faith in God provides for them. I remember one incident of a man who had delivered a big load of soft drinks like Coca-Cola. He was relaxing before making another trip to pick up more soft drinks. They drink a lot of these drinks in Nigeria and I noticed the same in Kenya and Uganda. The driver was sitting in the cab of his big semi truck. I greeted him and asked him what he was reading. To my surprise and edification he said, without any embarrassment and with a friendly smile, "I am reading my Bible."

If I have a little extra money I will help old friends and new ones with paying a hospital bill for a sick child, or an education bill for better schooling or to start a small business. I keep remembering my secretary Bea from my days at the Church of St. Matthew and the days of the fire and building the new church. With her limited means she always impressed me with her generosity. She modeled generosity for me. I keep learning over and over again by following her example. God is never outdone in generosity. If you do not believe me, try it and see. My work at the Faith

Joseph Gotau and his wife Francisca are dear friends living in Jos, Nigeria. Joseph works for the Carter Foundation (Founded by former President Jimmy Carter) in Jos.

Alive Clinic is some counseling. Besides this Dr. Chris is encouraging me to help get AA more alive. Alcohol and the anti-viral drugs some are taking do not make a healthy marriage. We have so many AA groups available in the USA. You are lucky to find one in all of Africa. So there is not much support for his patients who also live with the disease of alcoholism. My work in Jos has been in that area with some teaching of the *Aware Ego* and Voice Dialogue process. My dream would be to get some dedicated AA or NA people from the USA to come over and start and empower some strong and vital groups both here and in Uganda.

My travel to Johannesburg has been more in the area of teaching about the Theory of the *Aware Ego* and the process of growth available by Voice Dialogue. Brige, Nellie and Leslie, as I mentioned, have been working to make this work more known in South Africa. Ethne who is very involved in the leadership of Centering Prayer Communities has seen the need for this education to help them grow in so many ways. The seeds are being planted. We let God do the growth and the bearing of fruit. The harvest will happen. Being a Catholic Priest, along with being Bill Whittier, alias Fr. Gulliver, a teacher in promoting the message of AA begun by Bill W., and being an *Aware Ego* in process spreading the work of Hal and Sidra Stone, all have provided different ways for me to contribute to

Joseph's older brother Peter Gotau and his wife Catherine also living in Jos, Nigeria. Peter works at the Archbishop's House in Jos.

peoples' Journey. I may sound like a broken record but it is the journey we are all on to find ourselves, to find our own wisdom and to find our God. As we do this with God's generous help we change ourselves and change the world.

Kenya was more the focus on teaching about addiction and helping the teaching of AA to bring healing and joy to the lives of persons living with addictions. I lived with Denis and Ebby in Mombasa. Mombasa is primarily a Muslim community. It is also a tourist haven since it is on the sea and the eastern seaport of Africa. MEWA Rehab in Mombasa needed new life. MEWA is a large Muslim organization and the letters mean Muslim Education and Welfare Association. The Rehab was only one part of the work of MEWA. With Denis's leadership and my help along with the staff coming alive and being trained we upgraded the Rehab. The recovery that we called to life is still going on and is very much alive. Many of the clients for the rehab come from the Muslim island of Zanzibar. I enjoyed these guys and wanted to visit Zanzibar. I got my wish just before I left for India. Zanzibar is a very fascinating island with much tourism. I bargained with one of the young clients from Zanzibar to give me his sandals in exchange for a recovery book. I am still wearing these sandals today. They carry his energy and remind me of him and Zanzibar. I wanted to encourage and be involved in getting a rehab started in Zanzibar. Inshallah, I will leave this to my successor to help with this project. Three persons I still have regular contact from Mombasa continue to do good work in keeping recovery alive and well. Solomon who I call "King Solomon" is a recovering alcoholic working and doing continual training in spreading the message of recovery. He calls me his son and I am honored. Ahmed is very involved in MEWA and on their board. He continues to dedicate much of his energy for calling addicts and alcoholics to recovery and supporting them to be faithful to their recovery journey. Then there is Suleiman from Zanzibar a recovering addict doing fantastic work against great odds in bringing recovery to Zanzibar.

This was my first experience living and working with a Muslim Community. I was touched and impressed with their dedication to God and care for each other. One day traveling home from the rehab in the local mutates (small buses for local transportation), a veiled Muslim mother and her two young children sat next to me in the front seat. I choose when possible the front seat, since entering and getting out is easier for a young man like me. In addition to this benefit there is more

Entrance to Faith Alive Clinic in Jos, Nigeria. Patients are lined up waiting to see the doctors.

room and I could see well. With this friendly veiled Muslim Mother sitting next to me with her children, a further awareness came home to me. These Muslim mothers and families are like all families around the planet. They are struggling to raise their children, educate them, stay in love with God and be happy with their lives and with their God. At this same time there was much propaganda on the local TV claiming how terrible the Muslims are. It was a dishonest attempt to justify the invasion of Iraq.

My service in Uganda will again be focusing along with Father Sam Mwaka on building AA support communities in the villages. The long range plan would be to provide a suitable rehab to meet the needs of persons living there with addictions. But a rehab is very expensive to begin and sustain and needs AA and NA communities that are alive and well.

Dr. Chris and his children and wife Mercy and woman on left helps with children.

They provide the needed support for those coming out of rehabs to continue their life long journey of recovery. Stay tuned for the next chapter where I will explore with you in more detail my visit to Uganda.

Fr. Bill visiting Fr. Sam's home village in Kalongo, Uganda.

CHAPTER TWENTY-ONE

Off To Uganda

"Come Follow Me."
2008-2009

One morning I received a phone call to help with a daily Mass at Church of the Immaculate Heart of Mary in Minnetonka, Minnesota. I was not too excited to go but I did say yes and went. Who do I meet at the church before Mass but a daily Mass worshiper Pete Truax? Pete is offering hospitality to Fr. Sam Mwaka from Uganda. Fr. has come to Minneapolis to get excellent medical care for a hip replacement, which had not been done correctly in Uganda. With our visiting that morning Pete became aware of my work with Alcoholism in the Third Word. A light went on for Pete. He told me Fr. Sam is not only recovering from hip surgery but is a recovering alcoholic. He is not only an alcoholic but he also is very committed to developing AA and other means of combating alcoholism in Northern Uganda. Pete invited me when I was free to come to his home and meet Fr. Sam. I did accept his invitation to visit and I met Fr. Sam. He shared with me that because of the war and the government driving the villagers out of their homes, alcoholism is rampant in northern Uganda. In the midst of our

Fr. Bill In Fr. Sam's Home In Kalongo

visit and seeing my interest in recovery, Fr. Sam said, "Come follow me to Uganda." I had to check my calendar and also make sure the two requirements—a western-style toilet and water I can drink—were available. They were met. Checking my calendar I noticed I was doing some recovery work in the Manila area in September and October. I was then coming home from the Philippines on the day we celebrate Thanksgiving Day in America. With a little breather I saw I could come to Uganda on December 12th and then on to Nigeria on February 11th. I had not planned on Uganda before Nigeria, but I was open to help Fr. Sam. I said December and January will work for my visit. Fr. Sam said excellent.

Fr. Andrew Kalawa on the left, myself, Bishop Sabino, and Fr. Sam on the right at the Priest's Annual Retreat providing education on addiction.

His Grace Archbishop John Baptist Odama (not Obama) sent me a cordial invitation to come to Gulu to help promote sobriety in the Gulu Archdiocese. He mentioned because of the 22 years of insurgency and internal displacements in the camps, the people of the Archdiocese of Gulu have been gravely affected by alcohol abuse.

With this invitation, on December 11, 2008, I boarded the NWA flight leaving at 3:20 p.m. for Amsterdam and arriving in Amsterdam at 6:30 a.m. on the 12th. This was an 8-hour flight. Then at 11:00 a.m. the same morning, I boarded the KLM flight to Entebbe in Southern Uganda. After another 8-hour flight, I arrived in Entebbe on Lake Victoria at 9:00 p.m. Father Tony Wach a Jesuit friend met me and drove me to their house in Kampala. The next day Fr. Tony drove me to Gulu in the north.

So I am now in Uganda on December 12th. This was my first visit to

Uganda. I would be celebrating Christmas here. I enjoy celebrating Christmas in different countries where I can experience the different customs of celebrating. The added plus for me in traveling in December is it is a wonderful way to avoid our severe winters in Minnesota. I also with no sadness escape the "crazy consumerism" of the Christmas season in USA. My age is showing. We celebrated Christmas in Kalongo, east of Gulu which is the original home of Fr. Sam. We traveled in his pickup truck. He and I were "going home for Christmas." I noticed and commented that the decorations for Christmas were very simple in the parish church. I expected such in a poor country. The central focus for the Christmas decorations was the Christmas crèche or crib with baby Jesus and Mary and Joseph. I also mentioned to my surprise that baby Jesus was not black but very Caucasian. Being Jewish the historical Jesus was not as white as this baby was. As I think of it most of our baby Jesus statues are equally as white in the USA. The morning after, we were offering Mass with the Sisters in their Chapel. I asked the question to the Sister who was kneeling next to the crib why Jesus was not black. She immediately responded that black is from the devil. Almost as quickly as these words escaped her mouth I could see her look at herself and realize she was black. From her I learned that the early missionaries to Uganda taught the natives that black was from the devil. This struck me strange when the missionaries were working with such beautiful black people and inviting them to be Christian.

Our Christmas Mass in the main church was in the native language so it was a little difficult to follow but I did ok. After lunch with the Sisters, Fr. Sam and I had a unique experience for me. We visited his home village just outside the church compound. The village is made up of clay brick circular huts with grass thatched roofs and dirt floors. This is where the people lived and where Fr. Sam grew up. We walked amongst the huts and greeted the people sitting outside on the ground or on mats. We greeted them with "Apwoya," which is a local language greeting used for almost everything, including Merry Christmas. This access to the native villages was what I had not had much exposure to in my previous visits to Africa. I was usually more in the towns and cities. I was privileged to meet Fr. Sam's mother and some other of his family members in the village.

Back in Gulu I was staying in the Sacred Heart Seminary. Right outside the gate was a similar village where people had settled after they had been driven out of their own villages by the war or the government. Each morning before Mass I would take a walk outside the gate. I would see the village wake up and do my morning ritual of greeting the morning sun as our planet earth turned to welcome it. This was very different from taking a walk in our American towns and neighborhoods. They are usually very quiet and no people to be seen. As I

Sr. Evaline Nafuna At Lacor Seminary Gulu. Sr. Evaline Nafuna took excellent care of me and led me through the "musical rooms" exchange.

enjoyed this experience it made me appreciate all the comforts I had living in America. It also made me realize the loneliness in many of our neighborhoods in America. I marveled at how the villagers lived so simply. Their huts were small with no water or toilets inside. There would be no room for them as well. I also marveled how many lived in these small huts. The image came to mind of the Volkswagen at the circus with endless clowns coming out of a little car. Another thing that amazed me here and in other places I visited was how clean their clothes were especially the white ones, with no laundry facility to speak of. The villagers in early morning, mostly women and young children, smiled, waved and greeted me. Many were women standing outside of their huts nursing their young. Others both little ones and older ones were off to get water for cooking and washing from the local water bore hole. Many of them were bringing the heavy water containers back on their heads. I lifted one of these containers and I could not imagine how they could carry such a heavy container on their heads but they did. Close to the highway going to Sudan near the edge of the village was their outside toilet and bath facility. This was a small circular hut made out of mud bricks with no roof. When I was out walking, the little ones loved to come over and touch my white hairy arms. They would hesitate not knowing how I would react. When they saw it was ok they enjoyed it and laughed as children do. I enjoyed it too. Another sight for me was watching the little ones learn how to ride a large bicycle. They were too short to reach from the seat so they would straddle just above the chain. They struggled in the beginning and then did well and were happy. I would cheer them on. The main road or highway to Sudan was just in front of the Seminary and this village. Big trucks roared by day and night on their way to and from the Sudan. Along with the noise, dust was always flying in the air. Potholes were a plenty as well. When I traveled with Fr. Sam we traveled in his

Fr. Bill with participants in the Seminar on addiction in Gulu.

open-back pickup truck. I was lucky and got to sit in the front. Others who traveled with us sat in the back, which was not only bumpy but very dusty. At my young age and used to my USA comforts, I never could have handled the back. The locals handled it well and were happy to have a ride. Bicycles were a common mode of travel for many besides walking or riding in the back of trucks. Even here I was amazed how much they could carry on a bicycle. I noticed this same phenomenon in India of how much you can carry on a bicycle, if you know the trick. Women walking would have their baby on their back, something else on their head and their arms loaded as well.

There was a village behind the seminary. I would walk down there to enjoy the walk and visit the people and experience their lifestyle. Not all knew English. Some of them knew enough English so I could visit with them. On one of my visits I noticed smoke rising above the high grass and a large square pile of bricks. There were young men feeding the fire under the pile of bricks. This was a kiln and inside they were baking bricks they had made from the local clay. These bricks were used to build the walls of the huts they lived in. If those who made the bricks did not need them for their own use, they would be sold for some income.

Standing by the kiln and helping feed the fire was a friendly young man who caught my attention. He also knew some English. His name was Ocora, Ronald. The last name was first. After visiting some, when we both became relaxed I asked to see his hut and meet his grandmother who had raised him. He had lost both his father and mother when he was very young. This parentless children phenomenon was quite common in Africa. With the AIDS epidemic Grandmothers raising their parentless grandchildren is becoming very common.

Ronald and I became instant friends and from this ongoing friendship Ronald became my Black Son and I became his White Father. Here is another self named. He was smart and I encouraged him to go for more education. He did not have money for that so I offered to help my black son to attend computer classes in the village. I always would tell the young people I met to learn English and learn how to use a computer. This skill and knowledge will help you get a job and make a future for yourself. Ronald has been taking computer classes and has learned how to use the internet. This allows us to communicate on a regular basis now that I am back home in New Hope, Minnesota, USA. I need to encourage him to keep writing and learning more English which is weak for him.

Father Sam and his PACTA staff organized an education seminar on addiction for about 30 people from all walks of life. He and his staff saw the need for more education. My visit helped to create more interest in the Seminar. I would be the main presenter. I introduced the topic of the Seminar. I did some teaching of the Psychology of Selves to show how the selves—like Pusher, Pleaser, Perfectionist, Critic and Rational Mind—when too big or disowned, can be part of the cause of addiction. Education is needed to understand that a person living with alcoholism is not a bad person who needs punishment. He or she is a sick person who needs healing. It never ceases to amaze me how much ignorance there is all over the planet on this basic truth about the disease concept of addiction. Besides education there was a need to build up AA Groups and other means to remove the scourge of alcoholism. Alcoholism was destroying lives and families and homes. This was creating even more poverty in the villages. Since the villagers were driven off their land they had no work. This idleness was part of the creation of alcoholism especially among the men.

Since the priests are significant leaders in the villages we saw the need for some education and motivation for them in supporting recovery. Fr. Sam and I, along with Msgr. Matthew and Bishop Sabino, provided some education on addiction at the annual Priests' Retreat. The priests responded with interest and questions. They saw the need for their pastoral leadership in supporting recovery in the villages. Inshallah, God willing, if I return in December we, meaning myself and the PACTA staff, will do education in all the villages and work on setting up local AA groups. This will be a real challenge and if any of you who read this want to help you are most welcome.

Have you heard of the game of "musical chairs"? I had something similar and I call it the "musical rooms."

When I first arrived Sister Evaline gave me a newly furnished room a little distance from the office and dining area. When it came time to eat it was so dark I could not find my way to the dining area. I had forgotten to bring a torch for seeing at night. So on my first night there, I did not go for supper and they missed me. Fr. Sam came looking for me and discovered my problem. With his torch we got to the dining area. The next day Sister moved me to another room closer to the dining area with some outside light available.

Fr. Bill and Pacta Staff In front of The Office

The room was very adequate but then one morning I found what seemed like hundreds of white ants flying all around my bedroom. I had never seen anything like it before. I quickly closed my bedroom door to contain them. I called Sister Evaline for help. She came running. She was always so good about taking care of me. The ants, which had nested in the wall of my bathroom, came out for a visit. That night at dinner guess what was a delicacy on the table? Yes you guessed it, roasted white ants. I chose to pass on the delicacy to Monsignor Sebastian. Monsignor Matthew, Monsignor Sebastian, Fr. Eric and Fr. Sam ate with me at meals. Monsignor Sebastian loved the white ants so I told him he could gladly have my share. We had lots of fun at the dinner table. In good humor, I would pick on Monsignor Sebastian and he loved it. Sister Evaline came again to my rescue. The musical room game goes on. Sister put me in another room which was very adequate, but termites were eating away the window sill. As long as the window did not fall out, this was not that serious. It worked out well for me as long as the wind was not too strong. About that time another challenge came my way from this room. If I locked the door with my key on the inside I could not get it open with the key. So I called Sister Evaline for help again. If I slipped the key under the door she could open it from the outside. With this event I made the resolu-

Fr. Bill At Kalongo IDP Camp

tion not to lock my door from the inside anymore. About this time another thing happened to me. Someone broke into my email account and sent out an Emergency message to all those in my address book. The message indicated I was in Nigeria and I had lost my passport and money. I was in desperate need and needed $1800 to take care of my needs. Most people recognized it as a scam and those who knew me well knew I did not write in this manner. But everyone was worried and concerned. They still did not know for sure if I was in trouble. I was not in trouble and I was well taken care of in Gulu. I was not even in Nigeria at the time. Two friends from my condo here in New Hope responded to it with generosity not knowing it was not from me. They did not know who to call to verify if it was a scam from Nigeria. The money got sent and I felt the need to work out a way to repay them. They felt very bad and embarrassed about being taken in. I was edified with their care and generosity for me. So back in Gulu and the Seminary I was worried about this entire scam thing. I went to my room and forgot my resolution to not lock my door. Yes you guessed it, I locked the door and again, I could not get out. Lucky for me I had a cell phone I used locally. I had to call Sister Evaline or Father Sam to rescue me. Fr. Sam and Sister Josephine came this time. Such was the tale of my game of musical rooms at the Seminary. We had lots of laughs with the musical room's game. Do not let this tale scare you away from coming for a visit. You are well taken care of and always welcome. I am, Inshallah, planning to return in December. I made one selfish requirement for my return visit. I want to have Sister Evaline to be there to again take such good care of me. Unfortunately for me she has been transferred so I will miss her. If I return, part of my agenda will be to find her and have a good visit with her. The scam was serious and with poor internet protection in the Gulu area, this had happened to a couple of local priests earlier.

Before leaving Gulu to head for Jos, Nigeria, the staff at PACTA wanted to have a meeting with me to evaluate my visit. From my point of view it did not seem I had made much of a contribution. But their response was very different. They each shared with me how they perceived my visit and how much they appreciated my coming. It brought tears to my eyes. They wanted me back again. At this time I have a tentative commitment to return in December and help set up AA in the villages. Come and help me!

There is much more to share but this gives you a little picture of my visit. One outstanding quality of all the Uganda people is their spirit of welcome to their visitors like me and you. I told them at the Seminar, I think I learned more from them than they from me. But as is usually the case we all learn together and from each other if we are open. We all were open and learned.

As I close this chapter it gets me going back to my reflections on relationship as teacher and connector. I could see how many relationships, beginning with Pete at the church, brought about many important connections for me and for those I connected to in Uganda. Since this was a more recent visit for me I feel I have given you more details. Details are still in my memory. I have done so much of this traveling I tend to not talk about some of the details, forgetting that many of you who read this may enjoy and want to know the details. With this first visit I did not have time to enjoy Lake Victoria and the Game Park so Inshallah I will enjoy it on my next visit. If you want more details let me know via email. Also this book is not about soliciting funds but PACTA and their important work with helping alcoholics and addicts need all the help they can get. If you see this as something you want to support, you are most welcome to help. Again let me know by email.

Msgr. Matthew drove me back to Kampala and the Jesuit Retreat House. Again Fr. Tony drove me to Entebbe to catch a flight on Kenya air at my favorite time in the morning 5:10 a.m. (Only kidding). This took me on to Nairobi in Kenya. Then I made another connection on Kenya Air to Lagos. The flight was almost empty and they wanted to get the plane to Lagos which is a central hub for air travel in West Africa. Then after a long wait in Lagos, which is not my favorite airport, I made a connection with Virgin Air to Abuja in Nigeria. I was met by the driver from Faith Alive and the next morning we drove to Jos and the Faith Alive Clinic. The infrastructure for traveling by air in Africa is very poor. I remember the title of the James Bond movie "Never Say Never." I am warning you ahead of time if you decide to try my crazy schedule of travel in Africa, my recommendation is to say Never or NO.

The finish line photo of Fr. Bill running in
Grandma's Marathon at Lake Superior in
June 1983

CHAPTER TWENTY-TWO

Self Care on Our Journey
2009

Love Your Neighbor as you Love Yourself

On the morning of January 5, 2009, I woke up early from my bed in Gulu, Uganda. The message came to me that I needed to write a chapter for my autobiography on Self Care. This could be a separate chapter or added into one of the existing chapters. I decided to make it a separate chapter, so here it is.

Since we are a unity of mind, body, and spirit all three are part of good health care. As a young boy my mother, our health and physical education classes in school and my involvement in sports made me conscious of the importance of taking care of myself starting with physical health. I was not the star athlete in high school sports even though there was a self in me who wanted to be. From this interest I was aware of the importance of good physical care of my body. As a young boy I was somewhat conscious of being a little on the fat side which my critic self did not like. As freshmen at St. Thomas College we had, along with educating our minds and spirits, physical education classes. These classes enhanced my awareness of taking care of my body. At Nazareth Hall and the Major Seminary along with the education of our minds and hearts we had allotted recreation time for sports. I used this time for handball, racket ball, basketball, hockey, and football along with swimming.

When I was working in the parish besides taking care of my mind and spirit and nourishing relationships, I enjoyed being involved with the youth in basketball, racket ball and tennis. As I mentioned earlier, going to the lake when I was at Maternity of Mary in many ways saved my vocation and my health. I enjoyed volleyball. I enjoyed the many relationships in relaxing and having fun together. Along with this I learned and enjoyed water skiing and

Swimming in the ocean and love for the beach in Bradenton, Florida - thanks to Aunt Jane.

swimming. The swimming I had learned as a boy in the local Vermillion River in Farmington. Also while at Maternity Mary there was a Mission and I was not needed in the parish that week, Alleluia! I was blessed to visit my cousin for the first time in Bradenton, Florida. Aunt Jane as we called her was somewhat handicapped with arthritis and retired but she definitely was refired by the Spirit. She offered me grand hospitality. It was my first exposure to the ocean. From this I developed my love for the ocean and the beach. This love has continued to grow and now that I am younger this interest is not so great.

Thanks to Mary Maier and her family, I had a number of visits to Switzerland to bike and hike.

When I was at St. Matthew's I joined with the youth on Sunday afternoons playing basketball. We were blessed in having access to our own school gym. With others I played tennis and began downhill snow skiing. Moving on to St. Pius X, I continued with these sports in different ways and also enjoyed riding my bike. When I got involved with the Pastoral Education program at Hazelden, this reinforced my priority for self care. Recovery was a selfish program taking care of your whole person. If you did not take care of yourself no one else would or really could. Also this brought back into focus the great commandment of love which says "love your neighbor as you love yourself." If you cannot love and take care of yourself correctly how can you love your neighbor correctly?

When it came time to leave St. Pius X and go on to Los Angles to join Hal Stone for that year, I was faced with a question/decision. How will I continue to keep in good physical condition? There I will be in a new and big city not knowing anybody and without a bike. Running came to mind even though when growing up in high school I had no love or interest for track. So in preparation for leaving St. Pius X, another agenda item for me was learning how to jog or run in a healthy way. This I did gradually learn and I got into shape. I discovered this was an ingenious idea. I needed no equipment to speak of except shoes and did not need others to do it with. So off I went to Los Angeles. My daily agenda was an early morning jog for about 45 minutes very early in the morning. I think this was about 6:00 a.m. I wanted to avoid both the heavy traffic and the pollution which goes with it. At that time of morning pollution and traffic were at a minimum and you had silence and privacy which I enjoyed and needed. If my timing was correct I was gifted also to greet the sunrise each morning. While in Los Angeles I learned a very ancient prayer for greeting the sun and I still use it every day to this day. I share this prayer with you in both languages.

The Gayatri

"Om, bhur, bhuvah, swah; tat savitur varenyam; bhargo devasya dhimahi; dhiyo yo nah prachodayat."

This is the Sanskrit version.

Here is English version:

"O, Thou Who gives sustenance to the Universe, From Whom all things proceed, and to Whom all things return.

Unveil to us the face of the true Spiritual Sun, Hidden by a disc of golden light, that we may know the truth and do our whole duty as we journey to thy Sacred Feet."

I have memorized it in both languages and pray it in both while greeting the sun as our mother earth turns each day to welcome the sun.

What I have shared served me well for the year in Los Angeles. With my learning at the Center for the Healing Arts and before this at Hazelden, I continued to learn and walk the talk for good health. We need to take care of mind, body, and spirit and have healthy relationships. This would be Holistic or Wholistic Healing and Healthy living.

Back at St. Edwards my running continued to serve me well for good exercise along with good eating habits. One morning I met Jerry Gormley running in the park where I would run. I recognized him from seeing him at Mass on Sunday. Jerry was a regular runner. He even got me interested

Grandma's Marathon, June 1983

in training for a marathon. At this time I had left St. Edward's and I was in my first year at St. Bridget of Sweden. In my first year I had a little more time for training which I knew had to be a must for me. And yes training for a marathon takes lots of time. With the training I was amazed how well we can train our body and how far we can run with good training. Our goal was to train for Grandma's Marathon in Duluth. I know without Jerry's help, training, suggestions and inspiration, I would not have persevered to make it to Grandma's that spring. We ran the marathon. We both finished in good time with Jerry doing better than I did. But at the finish line listening and looking around at the gathering of runners, it came home to me that running to this extent is another addiction. Along with this I became aware of how much this training and running pushed one's body to the limit. I felt this was too much for a body I loved. My body was my best friend and I wanted it around for a long time. This was my first and last marathon. I was happy to have run it. The location at Lake Superior and the weather could not have been better. From then on an early morning run or jog was my daily agenda but only for about 45 minutes. While I was at St, Bridget's this served me well along with tennis playing, biking and both downhill and cross country skiing. When as Fr. Gulliver,

159

I started my world wide travels the regular daily early morning run served me well. There was little need for equipment. Most places were very hot even in the morning. I did not need someone else to do it with. So travelling light and getting sufficient exercise along with fresh morning air worked well for me. Out running early in these Third World countries made this white man from USA look a little strange, but I did not mind. As I got younger these last few years the jog has become a morning walk to serve the same purpose. With the guidance and teaching of my mentor Thich Nhat Hanh, I also practice Walking Meditation. His little book on walking meditation is a gem. I read a page every morning to give me added inspiration. The title is: *The Long Road Turns to Joy—A Guide to Walking Meditation* by Thich Nhat Hanh. The early morning walk continues to nurture my love and need for nature and often provides some ideal time for meditation and rosary praying. Along with this I continue to nourish my mind and spirit and relationships with good reading, teaching, counseling, and daily meditation. Along with all this Fr. Joe from Kripa has given me some Yoga postures and they have been very helpful for continued health and healing. These are my reflections on good Self Care. They have worked well for me and they may give you some hints for your life journey.

After writing this I was amazed how many varied activities I have been involved in to take care of my body, mind and spirit as well as nurture relationships and experience regular exposure to nature. This exposure to nature nourishes my spirituality by experiencing presence with love and awe the God of this magnificent universe. This universe of ours is our beautiful home and generous gift of our Beloved God. We are all blessed with having a God who lives in each of our hearts, in the entire universe and also transcends it. Yes, the best things in life are free.

Fr. Bill enjoying nature in Switzerland with a little lunch

CHAPTER TWENTY-THREE

Distinguished Alumnus Award
2009

A few years back, Kris Akin was working at the *Farmington Independent*, the local Farmington hometown newspaper. Kris had been receiving my Fr. Gulliver newsletters and passing them on to her mother-in-law, my cousin, Nancy Whittier Akin. Kris mentioned to her co-worker—Nathan Hansen (Editor) of the *Independent*—about writing an article about me as a former Farmington resident. I was now working worldwide and impacting people's lives spreading good will, help and hope for people dealing with addictions. Kris gave Nathan my website and he started to follow my travels and writings. Nathan eventually called me and set up an interview over the phone. The interview went very well and he invited me to send him some pictures. The article was then written up in the *Farmington Independent* dated February 28, 2008. Nathan titled the article "'Father Gulliver' helps people around the world."

A local Farmington school district employee, Aaron Tinklenberg, read the article and he was very interested in my work and travels.

Kris Akin, Fr Bill, Nancy Whittier Akin, cousins

Aaron is the school district's communications specialist. He also keeps in touch with FHS alumni with an email newsletter. Besides this Aaron also works with a non-profit organization that Kris helped start called the Farmington Area Education Foundation. The Foundation has a yearly awards program and fundraising dinner to celebrate education in Farmington and the students' and staffs' accomplishments. When it came time to start collecting nominations for the awards, Aaron told Kris he was going to nominate me. Kris affirmed that it was a great idea. They both felt my devotion and unselfishness in helping others, along with still working and traveling around the world, was an inspiration to young people and old people alike. The Distinguished Alumnus/Alumna Award is awarded to a Farmington High School graduate who has distinguished himself or herself through professional, social, or academic achievement thereby positively representing Farmington Area Schools to the broader community. I was honored to receive the award. I was not traveling out of the country so I attended the award dinner. With joy, humility, and gratitude, I received the awarded as a 1952 graduate of Farmington High School who was born, raised, and educated in Farmington. My cousin Nancy was able to be there along with her son David and his wife Kris. Also two classmates from Farmington with whom I have kept up our friendship these almost 75 years were able to be there and were honored to be there. Cletus Rotty who has become my personal photographer with his digital camera and John Devney were both there with their wives of over fifty years, Phyliss and Maryann.

The Statue of Liberty and Welcome in New York Harbor.

CHAPTER TWENTY FOUR

Concluding Reflections

2009

"We have only just begun."

We as individuals, church, country, and home planet earth have only just begun to find ourselves, our own wisdom and our God. As each of us and our world continues to make our life journey, some "maybe's" come to my mind and heart.

Maybe as a country we in America need to go back to our roots—The Constitution and Bill of Rights and own them and live them?

Maybe we as a country need to balance the opposites of freedom and responsibility, symbolized as Victor Frankl suggested with the Statue of Liberty in New York harbor and a Statue of Responsibility in San Francisco harbor?

Maybe we need statesmen and women rather than politicians who seek not the best for themselves and their party but work together for what is best for all the citizens of the United States of America and the World Community.

Maybe as a World Community we need to go back and own and practice International Law that respects human rights and brings about Justice for all?

Maybe as a Catholic Church we need to ask these questions:

1. Are we open to discuss that Vocations to the priesthood are out there with both celibate and married men and women but are not called?

2. Are we open to men and women serving as part-time priests with other professions?

3. Are we open to even limited commitments to priesthood and then after the limited commitment have choice to move on to another profession as is happening with our young people today. Many of our young people begin in one profession and then they return to school and move on to another profession?

A dear Religious Sister friend, Sister Thomasine, who has now gone home to God, reflected with me another insight about the possible shortages of vocations to the priesthood and religious life. She came from a large family and years ago our families were large and there were many children to choose religious life or priesthood or married life. Today our families are small and often consist of one or two or three children, whose

Sr. Thomasine

parents might like to have grandchildren rather than encourage their children to choose religious life. I hear young people say they would love to be a priest, but also be married and have children. Also there are many different ways to serve God today without being a priest or religious. Sister Thomasine's observations made sense to me.

Maybe we need to look more closely at developing Paul's teaching on the Risen Cosmic

Dear Father Bill,

Peace and all good as we continue to celebrate our beautiful Easter season!

Welcome home! It's been a long time. It's good to come back to your own culture.

I have been in Clare Residence (infirm) here at our Motherhouse since January! I can't seem to shake off what it is — perhaps my age (in my 89th year). I do have good days and bad days.

We are still having Winter weather even though officially we are in Spring. We are very grateful for all the moisture. Even our trees are saying "thank you."

I am eager to hear of all your adventures. You are a real pilgrim now. You must travel lightly also. How wonderful!

Even though you haven't heard from me, I have always carried you in my heart and prayer.

Blessings and love,

Sister Thomasine

169

Christ living in and embracing the whole universe? Teilhard de Chardin, John Main, Bede Griffiths, Ed Hays, Matthew Fox and others have only seemed to have scratched the surface on this reality and mystery of the Risen Cosmic Christ present in us and in our beautiful universe. In my judgment the best classic and scholarly book out today in this field is *The Coming of the Cosmic Christ* by Matthew Fox. I recently picked it up again off my bookshelf. I forgot and discovered to my surprise it was written back in 1988. Twenty years have gone by and not too many both in and of out of the church seem to be listening to this message. I realize Matthew Fox is held suspect by the Institutional Church. He is in good company with many of his predecessors. His predecessors like: Thomas Aquinas, Joan of Arc, Hildegard of Bingen, Meister Eckhart, Julian of Norwich, John of the Cross, my mentors John Henry Cardinal Newman, Teilhard de Chardin and so many others. All were pushing the boundaries of authentic spirituality and more progressive theology.

Maybe Jesus had more in mind and heart that the kingdom or church should be like Bill W. envisioned AA. There would be no commitments to lots of material possessions and political causes that hinder freedom and control the proclamation of the message of the Gospel?

Maybe the Christian Church needs to go back to its roots in Jesus and the Gospel? In doing this, to see what things are not in tune with the Gospel of Jesus and let them go. I sense many of these things distort and hinder the Church's image and ministry in our world today.

Maybe all the world religions need to go back to their roots and discover in the cave of the heart the one God of the universe and of all the world religions? In doing this we find the one God who loves us all in silence uniting us in love as one family of God.

My sense at this time in my life journey is that we as a country, church and home planet earth need to openly and honestly discuss the "Maybe's" I mention and others that I have neglected to mention.

With my limited experience in the Third World I could see an advantage for priests living in very remote villages to being married. Marriage would give them a partner to share life with and prevent (as happens in some cases) the unmarried priest choosing a woman for himself in the village. Marriage could also help some to not go to the bottle for escape from loneliness and other issues.

Also from my experience in the Third World where you have many convents of women religious, they become very dependent on a priest coming in from the outside. The priests often come at some distance and inconvenience to preside for Mass. Even like me they may get lost and come late. Why not an ordained Religious Woman in the community to provide this access to daily Eucharist for their community celebration of life and daily nourishment? When I mentioned this in one of the convents I visited in the Darjeeling area the Sisters reacted with joy and gratitude. Their response by word and expression was, "Oh Father may it come soon." I told them not to hold their breath too long.

For me being a celibate priest has worked well especially when I was younger and with my traveling as Fr. Gulliver. But as I have gotten older and my life more private, I miss more the intimacy of a partner to share life with. Also during my years in ministry I have always admired and been awed at how husbands and wives and their children take care of each other and support each other especially in serious illness and death. I have no partner or children or grandchildren to provide this for me. I see how my brothers and sister and other married friends had looked forward to grandchildren and now how much they enjoy them. The grandchildren enliven and add sparkle and joy to their lives. I do not have this added joy and sparkle and I feel the loss and loneliness. I also realize we cannot have all the options we might like in our life. With this in mind I feel the Church could be more open to allow more choices about who can become a priest and how priests live their lives and meet their needs for family and intimacy. With more priests available this would make for smaller, more vibrant, and faith-filled parish communities centered on and nourished by the Eucharist.

I have learned from Hal and Sidra the value of relationships and relationship as teacher. Since I am not in a primary relationship like marriage I do not have the opportunity to learn the lessons there for enrichment of my life. I see the need for sensual sexual intimacy in our lives as human persons. For me it is a challenge to know and set my boundaries for myself and for those I am in relationship with whether they are a man or a woman. I keep learning and sometimes I am a slow learner and make mistakes but I keep open to learn.

Father Gulliver's ship is feeling its age. The weakened sails cannot handle all the wind of the Spirit like they used to. The ship is showing its age in needing lots of updating and new life to continue its travels. Travel plans need reevaluation, and are being looked at. Father Gulliver needs to recognize and own his limitations for necessary self care. The little people are still out there all over our home planet earth and in our own back yards. They continue to call for and need justice and love, healing, care and food.

I love the truth as taught me by John Henry Newman. I see the need to be honest and generous as a necessary requirement for living the 12 Steps of AA. Honesty is a must for a joy-filled, ever expanding recovery and fully alive spiritual life. Saying this, I need to make this statement in truth and honesty. If I was a young man looking at priesthood today I would need to see very many necessary changes in the Church to attract me to say yes to becoming a priest.

Saying this I need also to say as I celebrate my 49th Anniversary of Ordination, which took place on February 19, 1961, that I have met many people who have enriched my life. I am blessed to have had the opportunity to enrich many of their lives. Along with this I have had a unique education flowing from that ordination event. Plus, all this without that event, there would be no autobiography and Fr. Gulliver's ship would have been stuck on land and never got to sail. I am grateful for all these blessings. The world today is very different from 50 years ago and much new vision, creative energy and courage are needed to bring the Gospel message to our changing and challenging world.

God's kindly Light has guided me well as it did John Henry Cardinal Newman and continues to do so. I would like to close with his poem or hymn with a little addition for clarity. Some of the expressions may need updating, coming from a different age and use of language. This prayer has been my daily prayer for years giving me hope and light in what oftentimes is a dark and scary world. With my work in recovery it is a good recovery prayer pointing up what is needed to be faithful in recovery and living out the 12 Steps of AA. The 12 Steps which I see are the essence, the core, and life blood of all the world religions.

LEAD KINDLY LIGHT
By John Henry Cardinal Newman

"Lead Kindly Light, amid the encircling gloom, Lead me on.

The night is dark and I am far from home, Lead Thou me on.

Keep thou my feet. I do not ask to see the distant scene; one step (at a time) is enough for me.

I was not ever thus, nor prayed that Thou should lead me on. I loved to choose my path, (and be in charge and make my own path) but now lead Thou me on.

I loved the garish day, and, spite of fears.

Pride ruled my will. Remember not past years.

So long Thy power hath blest me; sure it still will lead me o'er moor and fen, o'er crag and torrent, till the night is gone.

And with the morn (of reaching the other side of the kingdom) those angel faces smile which I have loved since and lost awhile."

Our Journey of Love goes on for each of us and for our
home and living space ship, Planet Earth

CHAPTER TWENTY-FIVE

Thank You

2010

I had written this chapter without the thank you title before I finished the other chapters. After rereading it too many times, I decided to not include it. But as happens to me on occasion an inspiration during meditation time came to me. The inspiration was to not omit it. Add some thoughts and make it a last sharing with those who have journeyed with me. In this spirit I have named this Chapter, Thank you.

My first sharing with you is this message from my heart. I want to thank you for taking the time and effort to make this journey with me. Some of the thoughts in this chapter if you have read the book will be a little repeat. However, they may provide some added hints for making your own journey of life. I remember this Latin phrase from my early days of school. "Repetitio est mater studiorum." The English translation is "Repetition is the mother of studies." So maybe some repetition will be helpful for you. It always is for me.

As I make my journey I keep growing and exploring and moving through life. As we keep moving our journey becomes more exciting and energizing as well as frustrating at times. These following thoughts or reflections surface in my mind and heart. They are not the last word but they keep encouraging and inviting me to keep exploring and allowing the process of the *Aware Ego* to grow and expand and deepen.

Life, Recovery and the *Aware Ego* process seem to me to be a journey to find ourselves, to find our own wisdom and to find our God. All of these in one sense are the same process. When we find ourselves, we find our own wisdom and we find our God as well. Since they are mystery they are difficult to get a complete understanding and grasp of. Our minds may be somewhat confused and even frustrated as mine is at times. Our heart knows we are going in the correct direction. This process or journey of exploration begins with our beginning. We all began as a vulnerable cute baby child. Remember how cute you were? This child carries our psychic fingerprint, our unique identity, as well as our vulnerability, our feelings, our emotions and our love connection with our God which I would call our spirituality. You may not recall your own childhood, but notice what we see as we watch and enjoy little children. We see their openness to life, their high trust level, their living and enjoying the present moment and their openness to the mystery of God all around them and in them. As the process or our life journey goes on, we grow up. In that process of growing up our vulnerable child and these other qualities get covered over and hidden. Many different selves develop to protect our child and these other qualities of life our child carries for us. It is called survival on planet earth. So our journey through life continues for us here on our home planet earth. The surprise is at the end of our life we end up where we started from. T. S. Eliot would say we know this place, ourselves and our God for the first time. The first time means as adults we are more aware of the mystery of life. We own our vulnerability. We know and express our feelings. We have a more grounded sense of who we are. We know and experience in our hearts the God of our Understanding. This is the one God of all the World Religions. God like truth has many different and sometimes surprising faces. Each world religion, each of us in our uniqueness, all of nature and the Holy Books of all the World Religions reflect some face or maybe a multitude of the faces of the one living God of this magnificent universe of ours.

My family and personal religion as a Catholic Christian provides many helps to empower and guide me on this journey. I need to be honest and admit it offers some obstacles as well. Each of the world religions provide certain helps, guides, rituals and laws to facilitate this journey of life. The 12 Steps of AA provide this for those in Recovery. These 12 Steps are not foreign to the essence of all the World Religions. As long as we live on the surface of these rituals and laws, we are very different in our approaches to make our love connection with God. Many of the misunderstandings between religions, and even fights and wars, take place at this surface level. My experience tells me that the more we just talk the talk of our religion we are disowning the deeper reality of God in our lives. So with this disowning or shallow spirituality we need to force our religious beliefs on others who follow a different path to the one God of the universe. It seems that in some way by forcing our religious beliefs and practices on others we convince ourselves we are right. Usually we are wrong or we would not have the need to force our beliefs and practices on others. As I often remark in some of my talks at the rehabs, we are all climbing the same mountain of life to find the God at the top, in our hearts and in the Mountain. If we were going to climb Mt. Everest which I have no energy to do, there are many different paths to reach the top. To make the climb, much training and discipline are needed. Base camps are needed and we would be crazy to travel alone. Following this metaphor, let us do the discipline we need to do for our inner journey. At the same time let us help each other climb the mountain of God rather than hinder and fight with each other along the way. Life and the journey up the mountain are too short, too challenging and too important. Why waste it bickering, competing, and fighting with each other. We sometimes are into even killing one another. The far better approach is to cooperate, collaborate, respect and inspire each other on the way. Then we reach the top with each other. Guess what? Moving up the mountain is like our inner journey into the cave of our heart. As we go beyond the surface and move with the discipline of prayer, contemplation and humble service to the cave of our heart, we discover we all are one. The Hindu expression is our God is one loving us in silence. As Paul says in Romans 5, our Beloved God is pouring forth love in our hearts by the Holy Spirit.

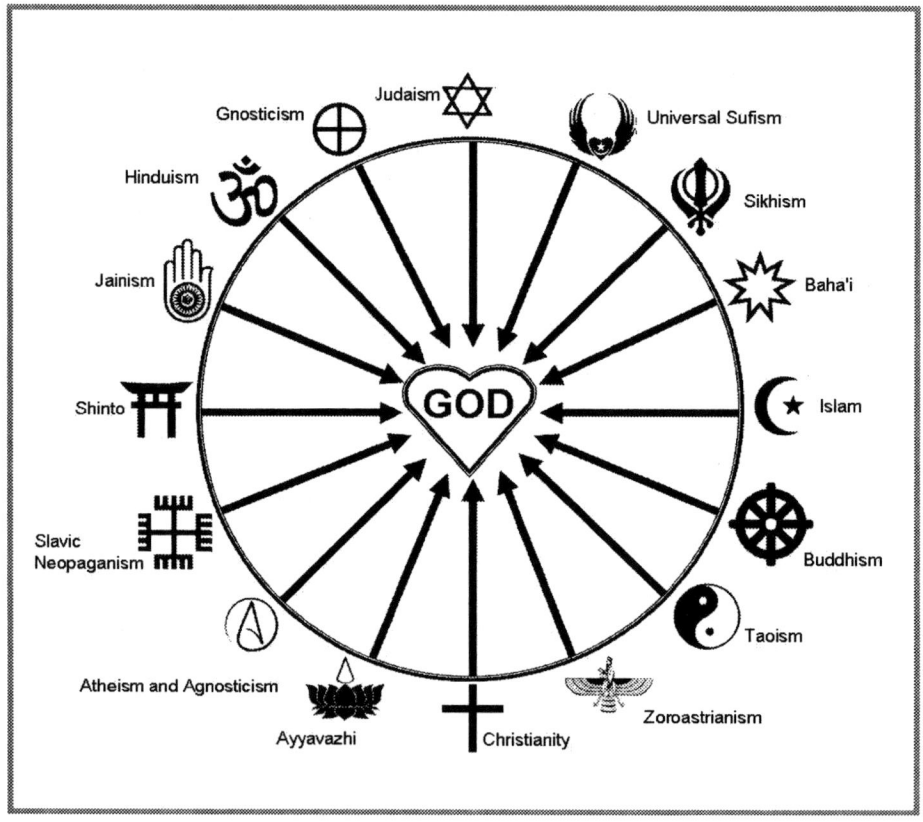

Another metaphor I like to use is a wheel with many spokes. On the outer rim of the wheel with each religion having their own spoke are all the different world religions. These include nature religions and the 12 Steps of AA. As long as we remain on the outer rim we are all very different, often superficial, living in our heads and disagreeing with each other. But as we move toward the center of the wheel, all these differences start to disappear. Instead of fighting with each other we begin to respect each other. We shift from our heads to our hearts. We can move toward the center in many different ways. The *Aware Ego* Process, specific religious rituals and practices that move toward unity are some ways. We can follow the 12 Steps of AA., meditation and contemplation disciplines and other spiritual practices to get to the center. We can lead humble lives of generous service. These are all different ways to move toward the center. As we practice and walk the talk of our spiritual tradition we let go of many of our differences. We discover the differences are not as important as we thought they were. Guess who we discover at the center of the wheel or the cave of our hearts? We discover the One God of this magnificent universe who our Christian Scriptures tell us is the Energy of Love This God-given universe is our beautiful home. We discover we are all one with that God in love and silence.

I have not been to the other side of the kingdom, but it seems to me our journey to find ourselves and our God and our own wisdom continues for us beyond the doorway of death. Hopefully on the other side of the doorway there is more light and love and wisdom to continue to move us along. Then one day we discover we are one with our Beloved God and one with each other in love.

Again thank you so much for journeying with me. May my journey give you some added hints on how to make yours. You may not agree with everything I have shared and that is ok. I close with the way I would close my newsletters and greetings when I traveled. I share some of my many selves with you beginning with Fr. Gulliver

Much Love and keep love circulating, it works,

Father Gulliver, Alias Fr. Bill, Sunshine, Kaka, Hippie Priest, Soul Lifter, Grandpa, Papa, White Father, Author, Counselor, Teacher and many other selves known and many more to be discovered.

P.S. My prayer for you who read this and all those who do not is that you would discover the "Gulliver Self" inside of you. Allow him/her to guide you to the little people who are longing to meet you. They may be far away in another country or continent or they may be right in your own home or next door or in your church and yes even in your own hearts. When you meet them with your heart, they will enrich and energize your lives beyond your expectations and bring you the healing and energy you need for your unique journey.

ADDITIONAL ENDORSEMENTS

THE AMAZING FR. BILL

How does one put in words what has been for me "a box of golden memories?" Since the first time I met our dear Fr. Bill in Hazelden in the year 1987 something made us feel that we belonged to the Lord for a very special mission. A long relationship has created many beautiful new beginnings for us as Persons, Priests and above all as Wounded Healers in the field of Addiction and HIV Aids. As Kripa Foundation, with the love support and inspiration of our Blessed Mother Teresa of Calcutta spread its wings all over India Fr. Bill lent his most valuable help. His presence was a soothing balm to many a desperate addict. With the teaching of Hal and Sildra, Bill made it so easy for our clients to experience the "Rore of Awakening."

As a fellow priest we shared a life of priestly care and concern for God's people. Many ex-clients remember Fr. Bill and long to see him and feel his loving warm embrace. The autobiography of Bill will show the reader how closely Bill's path and the Path of Kripa soaked in the presence of Mother Teresa blended together. We are deeply grateful to God for sending Bill like an Albert Schweitzer to the afficted of Addiction in India. May God bless him with a long life and well being.

With our love and gratitude,

Fr. Joe Pereira

Managing Trustee

Kripa Foundation

India.

ADDITIONAL ENDORSEMENTS

Dr Christian Ogoegbunem Isichei BM, BCH, MSc, FMCPath

I urge you as aliens and strangers in the world, to abstain from sinful desires which war against our soul.

Live such good lives among the pagans that though they accuse you of doing wrong, they may see your good deeds and glorify God on the day He visits us (1 Peter 2; 11-12).

These scriptural words confirm that we are all on a journey, on pilgrimage and the need to live godly lives.

For us therefore who are on this life journey, I would recommend my friend and mentor's book—Fr Bill's Life Journey. He shares with us the story of his life journey. In doing so he offers many useful hints for anyone else who is serious about life journey. Those who might find the book helpful are Christian Pastors and Laypersons, Doctors, Teachers, Therapists, persons interested in holistic health and healing, young or old members of all different world Religions, those in recovery or in need of recovery or any PERSON young or old serious about their life journey and their spiritual growth. I have been richly blessed not just going through the book but being closely associated with the author in different facets of life.

Dr. Christian Ogoegbunem Isichei BM, BCH, MSc, FMCPath

Founding Co-ordinator/Chief Executive Officer, Faith Alive Foundation, Nigeria (www.faithalivenigeria.org) and Associate Professor/Consultant Chemical Pathologist, University of Jos, Jos, Nigeria

ADDITIONAL ENDORSEMENTS
The Privilege Of Having You As A Friend

I first met Father Bill in 1989 when I was a patient at Hazelden in Minnesota. As a Catholic I was allowed to attend mass where Fr. Bill was pastor. We were not allowed much outside contact with the world when you're at Hazelden. This contact turned out to be unique for me in many respects.

Not many Catholic churches would have welcomed a bunch of addicts and alcoholics at there Sunday Masses. But this was a different breed of priest – one full of compassion and love for those who had hit bottom. He not only welcomed us but also praised us for coming. We weren't getting much praise anywhere else and it meant a lot.

As time progressed I got to know this priest better and better and was introduced to his concept of spirituality. This gave new meaning to the religion to which I was born into. I looked forward to each Sunday and his exciting sermons that almost always seemed aimed exactly at us. I was even more impressed that he would spend his free time with us at Hazelden. He truly was a "hippie Priest" in the nicest way.

As our Friendship progressed and we spent time at each other's domiciles we got to know each other better and better. He has been an inspiration to me that helped me transition from the work as a scientist to one as a psychologist. He was a great help to me in overcome my addiction and eventually to be able to help others with theirs

There are so few truly good and gifted men in our society that I feel it a privilege to call Father Bill my good friend. I've nicknamed him the "catalyst" since he gets so many people and things to change. His "catalyst" self also empowers him to keep growing and changing. I am thrilled that he was able to chronicle his life and work for us in this book.

With Much Love

Leo Kominek, PhD

A Prayer For Wholeness And Health

A Revised prayer for Wholeness and Health from my 25th Anniversary of Ordination

"The Risen Cosmic Christ lives in me." Gal.2:20

In my heart there exists a pure and powerful love energy which is the source of my life -

The Risen Cosmic Christ.

I now acknowledge and honor the Risen Cosmic Christ

For my mind, my emotions and my body.

May awareness, intelligence, and skill dominate my mind, canceling erroneous and limited thoughts.

Let my mind express wisdom and enlightenment.

May goodwill, joy and forgiveness fill my heart, dissolving fear, doubt and anger.

Let my emotions express understanding and compassion.

May vitality in form and function enter my body, restoring it to wholeness and waking it to action.

Let my body express productivity and passion for life.

May the energy of the light and love of the Risen Cosmic Christ surround me and renew and transform my mind, my heart, and my body.

Let my purpose in living be fulfilled.

Let my triumphant spirit radiate health through all that I am and all that I do.

I pray in the name and love energy of the Risen Cosmic Christ, my Beloved.

Amen

THE TWELVE STEPS OF
ALCOHOLICS ANONYMOUS

The relative success of the A.A. program seems to be due to the fact that an alcoholic who no longer drinks has an exceptional faculty for "reaching" and helping an uncontrolled drinker.

In simplest form, the A.A. program operates when a recovered alcoholic passes along the story of his or her own problem drinking, describes the sobriety he or she has found in A.A., and invites the newcomer to join the informal Fellowship.

The heart of the suggested program of personal recovery is contained in Twelve Steps describing the experience of the earliest members of the Society:

- We admitted we were powerless over alcohol—that our lives had become unmanageable.

- Came to believe that a Power greater than ourselves could restore us to sanity.

- Made a decision to turn our will and our lives over to the care of God as we understood Him.

- Made a searching and fearless moral inventory of ourselves.

- Admitted to God, to ourselves and to another human being the exact nature of our wrongs.

- Were entirely ready to have God remove all these defects of character.

- Humbly asked Him to remove our shortcomings.

- Made a list of all persons we had harmed, and became willing to make amends to them all.

- Made direct amends to such people wherever possible, except when to do so would injure them or others.

- Continued to take personal inventory and when we were wrong promptly admitted it.

- Sought through prayer and meditation to improve our conscious contact with God as we understood Him, praying only for knowledge of His will for us and the power to carry that out.

- Having had a spiritual awakening as the result of these steps, we tried to carry this message to alcoholics and to practice these principles in all our affairs.

Newcomers are not asked to accept or follow these Twelve Steps in their entirety if they feel unwilling or unable to do so. They will usually be asked to keep an open mind, to attend meetings at which recovered alcoholics describe their personal experiences in achieving sobriety, and to read A.A. literature describing and interpreting the A.A. program.

A.A. members will usually emphasize to newcomers that only problem drinkers themselves, individually, can determine whether or not they are in fact alcoholics. At the same time, it will be pointed out that all available medical testimony indicates that alcoholism is a progressive illness, that it cannot be cured in the ordinary sense of the term, but that it can be arrested through total abstinence from alcohol in any form.

For further explanation read the BIG BOOK of AA and contact a local AA Group in your area.

"The Spirituality of AA is not a Religion and seems to my mind and heart to express the core values of all the World Religions and their Spirituality".

Fr. Bill

The Twelve Steps are reprinted with permission of Alcoholics Anonymous World Services, Inc.("AAWS")Permission to reprint the Twelve Steps does not mean that AAWS has reviewed or approved the contents of this publication, or that AAWS necessarily agrees with the views expressed herein. A.A. is a program of recovery from alcoholism only—use of the Twelve Steps in connection with programs and activities which are patterned after A.A., but which address other problems, or in any other non-A.A, context, does not imply otherwise.